PENGUIN
SPECIALS

Penguin Specials fill a gap. Written by some of today's most exciting and insightful writers, they are short enough to be read in a single sitting – when you're stuck on a train; in your lunch hour; between dinner and bedtime. Specials can provide a thought-provoking opinion, a primer to bring you up to date, or a striking piece of fiction. They are concise, original and affordable.

To browse digital and print Penguin Specials titles, please refer to **penguin.com.au/penguinspecials**

LOWY INSTITUTE

The Lowy Institute is an independent, nonpartisan international policy think tank. The Institute provides high-quality research and distinctive perspectives on the issues and trends shaping Australia's role in the world. The Lowy Institute Papers are peer-reviewed essays and research papers on key international issues affecting Australia and the world.

This Lowy Institute Paper forms part of the Global Economic Futures project, which was made possible by a generous donation from Manikay Partners to the Lowy Institute in 2018.

For a discussion on *Reconstruction: Australia after COVID* with John Edwards and leading commentators on the economy, visit the Lowy Institute's daily commentary and analysis site, *The Interpreter*: **lowyinstitute.org/the-interpreter/debate/reconstruction-australia-after-COVID**.

John Edwards, a Lowy Institute Senior Fellow
and an Adjunct Professor at Curtin University's
John Curtin Institute of Public Policy, is a
former member of the Reserve Bank Board.
He was a senior economic adviser to Prime Minister
Paul Keating. His six nonfiction books include
Keating: The Inside Story and *John Curtin's War*.

LOWY INSTITUTE

Reconstruction

A LOWY INSTITUTE PAPER

JOHN EDWARDS

PENGUIN BOOKS

UK | USA | Canada | Ireland | Australia
India | New Zealand | South Africa | China

Penguin Books is part of the Penguin Random House group of companies
whose addresses can be found at global.penguinrandomhouse.com.

First published by Penguin Books, 2021

Typeset by Midland Typesetters, Australia

Printed and bound in Australia by Griffin Press, part of Ovato, an accredited
ISO AS/NZS 14001 Environmental Management Systems printer

 A catalogue record for this
book is available from the
National Library of Australia

ISBN 978 1 76104 277 5

penguin.com.au

For Canon John Morgan AM, whose friendship has been a treasured stimulus and refreshment over many decades.

CONTENTS

Preface I

1. Before the pandemic 5

   Australia's long boom 5

   The global economy 22

   China and the United States 33

2. The pandemic 45

   The human cost 45

   The economic impact 58

   China and the United States 73

3. After the pandemic 79

   The global economy 79

   Australia 85

   The United States, China and Australia 96

Conclusion 115

   Is globalisation dead? 115

   The idea of order 117

   Reconstruction 121

Endnotes 131

Acknowledgements 155

Preface

In the third decade of the twenty-first century, Australians find themselves in a strange place. Until the coronavirus pandemic, nearly two thirds of Australians had never experienced an economic slump in their working lives. Indeed, nearly half were not yet born or not resident in Australia when the economy had last tipped into recession, in 1991.

For most Australians, the savage economic shock of the pandemic and the subsequent troubled recovery have been the first sustained, widely shared and adverse interruption to their working lives in what was otherwise almost thirty years of unspectacular but sustained prosperity.

Incomes today are lower than they were before the pandemic. Many more Australians are jobless. Government debt is much higher, and much of it is held by the central bank. Decades after the float of the Australian dollar freed the Reserve Bank to manage the economy, power is shifting back to the Treasury. After three decades thriving in a congenial global economy, Australia now finds the world less congenial. Global growth is slower, America and China disagree about how the global economy should work, Australia is at odds with China, governments are deeply indebted, in many countries unemployment remains high, and global trade and investment seems more fragile than before the pandemic. The conflicting objectives of managing high government debt and the post-pandemic bulge in unemployment will preoccupy governments for the rest of the decade.

Yet many of the most alarming predictions for the post-pandemic world are already looking wildly overblown. Economic growth has resumed earlier than expected and, with very low interest rates and big household cash balances, is proving stronger than expected. Despite vast money creation by central banks, inflation is not now a problem and is unlikely to become one. Economic globalisation is not dead. On the contrary, cross-border trade is rebounding and the shared experience of the pandemic has made the nations of the world more conscious of their interdependence. America and China are at odds but have not decoupled their economies and are unlikely to do so. Though the global output loss due to the pandemic has so far been immense, the speed of recovery suggests the growth path of the world economy in a few years will be much the same as it might have been without the pandemic.

And while Australia's record-breaking run of economic success ended in the first half of 2020, it was not terminated by any fault in Australia's economic structure or its economic policies. Australia can regain the prosperity it enjoyed before the pandemic, and exceed it. But this demands recognition of new obstacles, and some old ones. It demands a clear focus on reducing unemployment, managing the increase in government debt, and navigating through the competition between the United States and China to sustain Australia's commercial and strategic interests. To find the right path, we need to know where we have come from, where we are, and where we are going.

CHAPTER ONE

Before the pandemic

AUSTRALIA'S LONG BOOM

It was the worst month of the worst bushfire season Australia had ever recorded. In December 2019, the fires roared through native forests, timbered farmland and small towns. They incinerated houses and people. They burnt nearly 200 000 square kilometres — an area four times the size of Switzerland. Blown by westerly winds, the smoke could be seen and smelt in Chile and Argentina, 13 000 kilometres across the Pacific.[1] Dust and ash from the fires reddened New Zealand glaciers.[2]

Those of us living in towns on the south coast of New South Wales were told to make a fire plan. Leaves should be raked up, roofs cleaned, buckets and hoses readied to douse embers. We should pack an emergency kit with water, a flashlight, a small radio, bandages. It was a good idea to ready boots, a hat, a wool jacket, long pants. You had to plan where you would go for safety and how you would get there if the fire approached. Most people who were killed by fire, we were warned, died in their cars. Our plan was to run to the beach, a few blocks away.

That December we mostly talked about the fires. Each day, all day, the media were full of fire news. The ABC broadcast local fire news and emergency warnings. There was a phone app that advised if fires were near, and whether or not they were under control. On the south coast of New South Wales, a fire was usually near, and often out of control.

As the fires spread along the highway to Sydney, it was difficult to get into or out of our village. Police came from the neighbouring town to monitor the evacuation of the camping ground. Nearby Defence land, always open to visitors at Christmas, was gated and guarded. On New Year's Eve, the Currowan, Charleys Forest and Clyde Mountain fires to the west of us, each immense, joined up. There was a smoke haze over the east coast of New South Wales so persistent it filled our nostrils and infused our clothes with the smell of eucalyptus oil. Winds blew the ash out to sea, and the tides brought it back, coating the sand with the black residue of burnt gum leaves.

Roads closed. It was safer to stay than leave anyway. Though burning to the north, south and west of us, the fires did not reach our village. A fire to the south had been so big and intense that late one afternoon it created its own weather. The sky turned yellow and black. There was a storm of lightning, hail and sticky, black ash. It was as close as we came to the horror experienced by other communities ravaged by actual fires, but even this sudden, weird storm was scary and, in a strange way, disturbing. The natural world, the world of light breezes, warm days, clean sand and clear waters was also capable of showing an immense, hostile power. In a warming world it hinted at troubles to come.

The bushfires had followed drought, and after the bushfires came floods. By early March the fires had been doused by two weeks of torrential rains. Amazed by the fires nearby, we paid no attention when on 4 January the World Health Organization (WHO) tweeted that there was a cluster of pneumonia cases in Wuhan City, Hubei province, in the People's Republic of China. Investigations to identify the cause were underway.[3] There had been no deaths.

After drought, fire and flood, a plague.

As those bushfires swept through the forests in December 2019, Australians were well into the twenty-ninth year of uninterrupted prosperity. It had not been a dramatic boom. It had many different phases, and had often been thought precarious. Yet every year, incomes were bigger, production higher. More people had jobs. Accustomed to continuous prosperity, we no longer remarked on it. It was routine. By 2019, it had been almost 30 years since Australia's last recession, and two thirds of the population had never experienced an economic downturn in their working lives.[4]

Nearly three decades of unspectacular but sustained prosperity had changed the country in many ways — some good and some bad. The country's output had more than doubled. Incomes had increased one and a half times. Measured in constant US dollars, Australian average incomes had been behind those of the United States and Japan in 1991. By 2019 they were ahead.[5] A higher share of Australians were in the workforce in 2019 than had been in 1991. Prices had doubled in the past 30 years, but jobs on average paid three times more. Unlike in some otherwise comparable economies, the lowest paid had kept up with all but the highest paid.

Wealth had also increased astonishingly. An Australian who owned a home in Sydney in 1991 saw its value more than double in the first half of the upswing, and double again in the second half.[6] By December 2019, the median value of a home in Sydney was just under $1 million. Of course, if you did not own a home in the first place, it became increasingly difficult to buy one.

Largely due to compulsory national payroll deductions introduced not long after the upswing began, the value of superannuation balances had increased fourteenfold.[7] The value of shares held outside superannuation had increased eightfold. Over the long upswing, the average Australian's wealth in houses, superannuation and other financial assets had increased sevenfold, while real incomes had increased by half. The average Australian household's net worth had reached $1 million in 2018, and was still increasing.[8] Most Australians had less than the average. Others had a lot more. Over those 29 years the wealth gap had widened.

Past upswings in Australia had often run in parallel with upswings in the global economy, and more particularly with the United States. They had usually begun and ended at the same time as elsewhere, often for similar reasons.[9]

A distinctive characteristic of Australia's long upswing that began in 1991 was that it was largely independent of downturns elsewhere. The United States had two recessions — one of them very serious — during Australia's long upswing. In both cases it was widely said that Australia would soon follow, yet in both cases the Australian upswing continued. When South Korea and Southeast Asia tumbled into a debt crisis in 1997, Australia was expected to be hit hard. Instead, its upswing continued at a somewhat swifter pace.

It was not the fastest growth Australia had experienced over a thirty-year period — the years from 1945 to 1975 saw a bigger increase — but it was certainly the most consistent. It benefited from the magic of compounding. So far as we know, it was the longest uninterrupted upswing in Australian history since European settlement. Some comparable economies had grown faster, but over the period from 1991 to 2019 no other rich economy had matched the durability of the Australian upswing.

Many Australians believed the country's wealth was narrowly built on iron ore, coal mining and farm products. Yet, while mining was certainly important over the long upswing, increased mining output accounted for only one tenth of Australia's output growth.[10] Even in 2019, mining still accounted for only one eleventh of Australian output.[11] Already a small share in 1991, farming accounted for only one fiftieth of output in 2019.

By then the mining workforce represented only one fiftieth of total employment. Farming had dwindled from one twentieth of employment in 1991 to a little more than one fiftieth in 2019. The manufacturing workforce by 2019 was down to one fourteenth of the workforce — more than the share of mining and farming combined, but half of the share it had in 1991. All up the three industries accounted for one job in eight. The other seven were in something else.

Most of the gain in Australian output over the 29 years — nine tenths of it — was accounted for by the growth of services. In this respect, Australia was like most other wealthy economies. Australia's output was mostly services, its workforce mostly in services and its economic growth derived from services. This in turn meant that Australia's economic wealth was not in its iron ore mountains or coal deposits or in the quality of its farming soils, but in the quality of the education of its workers, in their access to technology, in their ambitions. In these areas Australia had done well. Since 1991, the proportion of young people completing school to Year 12 had increased, as had the number at colleges and universities, and those with formal trade training. The quality of the workforce had markedly improved.[12] Boosted by a high intake of migrants, Australia's population had increased faster than most other countries. Adding to these gains, the workforce had increased faster than population.

For most of the long upswing, Australia had run a large current account deficit with the rest of the world. The deficit was financed by an inflow of capital from abroad. In recent years, however, the value of exports of iron ore, coal and gas, and of education and tourism services have been so great that the value of Australia's exports have begun to exceed the value of its imports. In 2019, to general astonishment, the current account deficit had become a surplus. Australia had become a capital exporter. Driven by superannuation funds, in 2013 the stock of Australian equity investment offshore had for the first time exceeded the stock of foreign equity investment in Australia. One day, perhaps, Australia's total assets offshore would exceed foreign-held assets in Australia. Meanwhile, a solid inflow of foreign direct investment into Australia continued, despite claims that Australian business taxes were too high and its investment rules too restrictive.

By 2019, Australia was busier, better educated, more productive and wealthier. There were a lot more Australians, they lived in bigger cities and they were more diverse and more engaged in the world beyond Australia. There had been 17.4 million residents in Australia in 1991. By December 2019 there were 25.5 million. More than half of the additional population were migrants. In 2019, nearly a third of Australians were born somewhere else — a share far greater than in Canada, the United States, New Zealand or the United Kingdom. In 2019 the share of foreign-born Australians was higher than it had been since 1893 — before the depression of the 1890s, the Great War and the Great Depression had slowed migration from the United Kingdom and Europe.[13] With little of the resentment and antagonism evident elsewhere, Australia's population had become considerably more diverse. In 2019 migrants from England were still the biggest group of foreign-born living in Australia, but they were nearly matched by migrants from mainland China and India.

Australia's outlook had changed. Since 1991, eight million Australians had been born, and over four million more people had migrated to Australia than had migrated from it. Four million had died. The generation that had seen the Second World War, and experienced the extraordinary post-war boom before the disappointments of the 1970s, was fading out by 2019. Even its successors, the post-war baby boomers, were growing old and ceding authority to the next generation. Prime Minister Scott Morrison, excoriated for holidaying in Hawaii as the bushfires burned through south-eastern Australia in 2019, was just four years old when Gough Whitlam's Labor government ended 23 years of Liberal Party rule. He was too young to have any memory of the Vietnam War, the Beatles and the Rolling Stones. He began his working career only a few years before the long upswing began in 1991. Like most Australians who had spent all or most of their working lives in an expanding economy, for Morrison prosperity was normal.

Once one of the most egalitarian societies in the world, and still one where people customarily addressed each other by their first name and bristled at any hint of expected deference, Australia had over the long boom become less equal, particularly in wealth. The extraordinary growth in house prices had increased the gap between those who could afford their own home and those who could not. The rapid rise in the premium paid for education and skills, the removal of arbitrated wages, and the much more rapid increase of bargained wages than award wages had contributed to greater disparity in incomes.

Though less equal, in the decade prior to the pandemic the tendency to inequality in incomes had been arrested.[14] And inequality remained much less than in the United States or the United Kingdom. Australia was in the middle of the Organisation for Economic Cooperation and Development pack — a little less unequal in income distribution than Japan, Italy, South Korea or Spain; a little more unequal than Germany, France or Canada.[15]

Unlike the United States or the United Kingdom — the two biggest 'Anglosphere' nations with which it was often grouped — Australia was not convulsed by the resentments of those whom prosperity had passed by. The top fifth of households by income in 2017/18 received four tenths of Australia's total income, while the bottom fifth received one twelfth. Since this had been so for a quarter century, it suggested that income growth for the bottom fifth had kept up with income growth for the top fifth — an unusual pattern among rich economies.[16]

Already wide before the 2008 global financial crisis (GFC), wealth disparities increased after it. In 2017/18 the wealthiest fifth of Australian households owned just short of two thirds of total household wealth — an average of $3.2 million a household. The bottom fifth owned just 1% of total household wealth, an average of $35 200 apiece.

The average at the top was 92 times the average at the bottom. Wide as the disparity was, the share of wealth owned by the wealthiest 10% of households in Australia was less than most OECD members. At 46.5% it was a little over half of the share in the United States, and under that of the Netherlands, Denmark, Germany, France and New Zealand.[17]

It had been a good run, but by the end of 2019 Australians had reason to wonder whether their circumstances were quite as satisfactory as they had been. Wealthier than ever in their history, better educated, with higher average incomes than their parents or those in all but a half-dozen other countries, living in a society that for all its ethnic diversity remained more harmonious than most, there was nonetheless a sense that things were not quite right. After many years of uninterrupted prosperity, a record unmatched by any country to which Australia could sensibly compare itself, living standards for most people were no longer improving as they had in past decades.

In the ten years to 2008/09, average income per head after inflation increased by one fifth. In the next ten years, to the eve of the pandemic, it increased by only a tenth.[18] Ten year growth to 2018/19 was the lowest since the ten years to 1982/83 — years that included the deepest recession since the Great Depression of the 1930s.[19]

It is not that things were bad in Australia at the end of 2019. Unemployment was around the average of the long upswing, living standards were higher than ever, taxes overall no higher than in America or Japan and much lower than in Europe or the United Kingdom, and government support for the poor was much the same as in other wealthy economies.

Prime Minister Scott Morrison would in 2020 recall the pre-pandemic economy as 'sclerotic'.[20] It was true that productivity growth had slowed, and with it the growth of output and incomes. Yet, after some years of vigorous debate, it was not easy to point to a problem in the economy that, if rectified, would restore growth to the pace of earlier decades.

Some argued that business investment was too low. Yet after removing inflation from both investment and gross domestic product (GDP), business investment as a share of GDP was twice as high in 2019 as it had been in 1991. Excluding mining investment, the level of real (or after-inflation) business investment in 2019 was at a record high.

Others pointed to high debt. There was no doubt about the rise in household debt, mostly to buy homes. It had reached 180% of household disposable income in 2019 — a formidable number.[21] But while household debt had never been higher, the interest rates paid on it had never been lower,[22] so the share of household income paid as interest on household debt in 2019 was the same as in 2002. For its part, business debt in 2019 was lower compared to GDP than it had been ten years earlier. Australian government debt had risen as a share of GDP, though by 2019 the increase had crested as deficits dwindled.[23]

And while the wages share of national income continued to decline (and the profit share to increase; a trend over decades), the drop was not as big as it appeared and probably did not show that owners of capital were appropriating an unfair share of productivity growth.[24] Some of the apparent change was due to the increased importance of the highly capital-intensive mining industry in Australian output.

Since employment growth increased while output growth declined in the six years to 2019, it is evident that the principal cause of slowing growth in real incomes, wages and output was declining growth in output per hour worked, or labour productivity. This decline in labour productivity growth was also apparent in other advanced economies. Its causes were not clear in Australia or elsewhere. As the Productivity Commission sensibly reported in early 2020, the slowdown was concerning but, 'such highlevel productivity measures rarely provide guidance to policy makers about specific problems to target'.[25]

The slowdown in productivity growth began in the mid-2000s in most advanced economies.[26] The Australian slowdown was less marked than most.[27] It was not uniform across the Australian economy. Industries such as mining, retail trade, recreation services and administrative services saw quite strong increases in productivity, while others such as agriculture, construction, and the electricity, gas and water utilities did not. It is evidently not an economy-wide problem.

The causes of the productivity slowdown were unlikely to include the level or structure of tax in Australia, or the structure of industrial relations, both of which had the same shape in 2019 as they had in the decade before the slowdown. Nor did research and development spending explain slower productivity growth.[28] No doubt there were improvements Australia could make in these areas, but there was no significant change that would plausibly improve productivity overall. The Productivity Commission reported in November 2020: 'It may be that there is less of a role for traditional "big bang" reforms, in favour of more tailored, targeted, and piecemeal changes.'[29]

Australia's experience in the few years before the pandemic was disappointing, but not wilful or easily explained. The remedies proposed were often and transparently ones that advantaged one interest group over another, without clear gains to the economy as a whole. There were no general signs of economic failure. Unemployment and underemployment were troubling, but well down on the highs experienced earlier in the upswing, while the labour force participation rate was near a record high. Though business investment overall was flat for the last three years of the upswing, non-mining business investment had risen to a reasonably high share of real GDP compared to previously. Household consumption had fallen a little as a share of GDP, though it had increased as a share of household disposable income. Wages growth was slow, but was close to productivity growth. Inflation was persistently below the target band for the Reserve Bank of Australia (RBA), but while that was a problem for the RBA as an institution, it was not of itself a problem for the economy. What is wrong, after all, with low inflation? There were certainly ways to improve performance in many areas of the economy, including industrial relations, federal–state relations, workforce training and health care funding and delivery. But even taken together, it was unlikely they would move the dial on overall productivity growth.

Towards the end of a difficult 2019, policymakers in Treasury and the RBA thought that things were getting better. Meeting in the eleventh-floor boardroom of its headquarters in Sydney's Martin Place in early December, the board of the RBA noted that interest rates were very low, finance for business was 'very accommodative' and Australian share prices were rising. Consumer sentiment had declined, which the board thought was associated with 'an increasingly negative tone' in the news coverage of the economy. Growth in Australia had continued at a moderate pace. The board was told that after 'a soft patch' in the second half of the previous year, the Australian economy had reached 'a gentle turning point'.[30]

At the end of 2019, Treasurer Josh Frydenberg, too, thought Australia was at a gentle turning point. Five days before Christmas, he announced that the 'budget remains on track to return to surplus in 2019/20'. Despite 'weak momentum in the global economy' and both drought and bushfires in Australia, forecast growth would be only a little slower than earlier expected. It would pick up to a projected 3% in a few years, while unemployment would fall to 5% of the workforce.[31] He forecast that by 2030/31 government net debt would be zero — an unusual achievement in a world of rising government debt.[32] Poised to complete the thirtieth year of uninterrupted prosperity, Australians in December 2019 had much of which to be proud.

Fifteen days after Frydenberg's budget update, the WHO office in China picked up from the website of the Wuhan Municipal Health Commission a media statement announcing local cases of a 'viral pneumonia'.[33] The first infections in Wuhan had been detected a week or so before the Treasurer's announcement.[34]

THE GLOBAL ECONOMY

The years of uninterrupted growth in Australia were also years of rapid globalisation. The separate economies of the world were becoming one. The modern global economy had begun during the Second World War with the creation of the International Monetary Fund (IMF), the World Bank and what would become the World Trade Organization (WTO). Based in Europe and North America, this global economy flourished until the mid-1960s, when the fixed exchange rate system on which it was based began to collapse under the pressure of rising inflation. A brilliant time for most industrial economies, the 20 years after the Second World War were followed by more than a decade of rising inflation, slowing and uneven growth, and higher unemployment — as evident in Australia as in other advanced economies.

Appointed chair of the US Federal Reserve by President Jimmy Carter and taking office in August 1979, Paul Volcker set about destroying inflation in the American economy. By 6 October 1979, he had assembled a sufficient consensus on the policymaking Federal Open Market Committee to sharply reduce the growth of money and increase interest rates. Two back-to-back recessions followed, but inflation came down from over 10% in 1980 to under 2% in 1986 — and stayed down.[35]

The Federal Reserve decision on 6 October 1979 was one of two sets of economic policy decisions made on the threshold of the 1980s that created the contemporary economic world. At the beginning of that same year, China and the United States established formal diplomatic relations. The economic opening to the world, which had been initiated by Deng Xiaoping the year before, accelerated in 1979 with special economic zones (SEZs) for foreign investment opened in Shenzhen and other cities. They would become the spearheads for China's emergence as a global manufacturing exporter. China opened to foreign investment, abandoned farm collectives in favour of private plots, and adopted a goal of creating a 'moderately prosperous' economy.[36]

By 1980 — a few years before Australia began its own period of economic reform — a new world was being created in which Australia would thrive. It was a world of moderate inflation, falling interest rates and increasing global trade and investment. China thrived, and the economic growth of East Asia far exceeded that of any other major region. In the 36 years between 1983 and 2019 — from the beginning of the low inflation era to the current pandemic — global output trebled and per capita GDP doubled.

Trade flourished. And although there had not been a global trade agreement since 1994, the number of regional or bilateral trade agreements rose from 50 to more than 280.[37] Exports of goods and services rose from less than a fifth in 1991, to nearly a third of global GDP by 2019.[38] Spurred by increasing trade and capital flows, global per capita income increased between 1991 and 2019 by more than in any 30-year period in history.[39] Increased output in China accounted for nearly a quarter of the total growth.[40] Australia's long upswing coincided with this global transformation.

Australia changed in ways that helped it fit into a more open world. In the 1980s and early 1990s, it floated its currency, sharply cut tariffs, lowered inflation and switched from arbitrated wages to bargained wages. It became one of the world's most open economies. In 1991 Australia had been party to a trade agreement with New Zealand. In 2019 it was still in the agreement with New Zealand, but also had trade agreements with China, the United States, Japan and South Korea. It was a member of a trade agreement based on the Association of Southeast Asian Nations (ASEAN), a member of another that also included Vietnam, Chile and Peru, and hoped to be party to a wider Asian regional trade agreement that included China.

Over those prosperous years, the global economy suited Australia. Australia's success was an exemplar of what globalisation could do. Australian exports rose faster than output as a whole. Foreign investment in Australia rose, as did Australian investment internationally. Australia freely imported new technologies from abroad and sold offshore some of its own. In the 30 years to 2019, Australian exports rose from one sixth of GDP to one quarter.[41]

For Australia, 'globalisation' was largely 'regionalisation', as it was for most countries. The nations of Western Europe became more integrated as the European Union. The United States, Mexico and Canada became more unified after the 1994 commencement of the North American Free Trade Agreement (NAFTA). East Asia became steadily more integrated as Japan, South Korea, Taiwan and Hong Kong shifted their labour-intensive production to China and ASEAN.

Australia's trade with East Asia grew more rapidly than its GDP or its trade overall. In the 30 years to 2019, the share of Australian goods exports sold in East Asia and the Pacific increased from a little over half to more than three quarters.[42] In 2019, more than one sixth of Australia's total income or GDP arose from its exports to East Asia. Half of those exports to the region were to China. By 2019, Australian goods exports to China were ten times those to the United States.

For Australia, the most enthralling and pertinent aspect of globalisation was the opening of China to world trade and investment, and its rise to become the world's biggest manufacturing economy. When Australia's long upswing began in 1991, China's economy was roughly the same size as Australia's. Japan — Australia's biggest customer at the time — had an economy ten times larger than both. By 2019, China's economy was nine times bigger than Australia's and nearly three times bigger than Japan's.[43] By 2019, China, Japan, South Korea, a number of Southeast Asian nations, Australia and

New Zealand had formed an economic community. The community accounted for more than half of the exports and imports of its members, and regional output was growing faster than any other. It was the most influential and spectacular change in the world economy over those three decades of Australian prosperity. The increase in goods exports to China accounted for roughly one tenth of the growth of Australia's nominal GDP over the whole upswing since 1991 — much less than widely believed, but considerable nonetheless.[44]

By the time the pandemic hit, Australia was meshed with China's economy — not only because China was the market for more than a third of Australian exports, but also because it was the major trading partner for Australia's other markets in East Asia. Thirty years before, more than a third of Australian goods exports went to Japan, South Korea and Taiwan — the economies adjacent to China (and the models for its development as an export manufacturer). As China's economy rapidly expanded, it became more integrated with its neighbours, and Australia's exports to China rose. Driven by the increasing importance of cross-border production chains, East Asia and the Pacific formed a regional economic community that, in terms of trade and investment between its members, was only a little less integrated than the European Union (EU), and far more integrated than the North American economic community.[45] Australia had become part of it.

In 1991 the RBA barely mentioned China in its public commentary on other economies important to Australia. Even 16 years later, China was included only among 'other trading partners' after discussion of the United States. But by November 2011, the assessment of China led the international section of the Bank's Statement on Monetary Policy, a change evident also in speeches by officials of the central bank and in the material presented to the board. By then, the RBA had posted economists to the Australian Embassy in Beijing and was known in the global central banking community for the quality of its reporting on China's economy.[46]

Like the Australian economy, the global economy in December 2019 was not quite as satisfactory as it had been. In the half century following the Second World War, international trade had always grown faster than world output. Capital flows between countries had increased faster still. Exports of goods and services were just 13% of world GDP in 1970 and 31% by 2008.[47] After the 2008 GFC, trade growth abruptly slowed, and so did cross-border capital flows. Cross-border trade accelerated from 2016, but it was 2019 before exports returned to the share of global GDP they had reached in 2008. Global cross-border financial flows remained well down on the levels reached before the 2008 crisis.[48]

In the rich countries, growth had decelerated since the GFC.[49] The growth of workforces had slowed or even declined, while the growth of labour productivity had fallen.[50] True of Australia, this slowdown in productivity after 2009 was also true of most wealthy economies, including Europe, the United States, Japan and South Korea. And while many possible explanations had been offered, none had been satisfactory.

China had accounted for a large share of global growth in the two decades to 2019. In the quarter century from 1991 to 2015, China's output increased tenfold, measured in constant US dollars.[51] By 2019, however, its growth had been slowing for nearly a decade. In that year it slipped to just over 6% — still more rapid than most economies, but slow for China.

China's economic structure had also changed. After decades of rapid growth based on very high investment, high savings and manufacturing exports, by 2016 the larger share of China's growth was coming from household consumption and services. Investment was still high and exports of manufactures still important, but in those years imports grew faster than exports and investment faster than savings. China's trade surplus with the rest of the world narrowed, and its current account surplus disappeared. Though its advantage had been in skilled, cheap labour, wages were rising so rapidly that in the manufacturing hubs they exceeded comparable wages in South America (Chile excepted) and were closing in on Eastern Europe's.[52] Some low-wage industries such as textiles and footwear were moving out of China to find cheaper labour in Bangladesh or Vietnam. To sustain growth, China needed to move away from assembly of product components made elsewhere to reach further back into the product supply chain. Intent on climbing the technology ladder, China gave more support to research and development and encouraged the growth of advanced technology industries.

Though it had slowed, the United States had grown faster than most other advanced economies. By December 2019, the unemployment rate was down to 3.5% — the lowest in half a century. GDP in 2019 increased by 2.3% — well below the 4% increase President Donald Trump had promised, but not far below the average of years since the 2008 recession. Demand had been sustained by company and personal income tax cuts in 2017 (at the price of higher deficits). After earlier tightening, the US Federal Reserve had changed course and begun to cut interest rates mid-year. Inflation remained under 2%. Like Australia's in 2019, the US economy was in the longest uninterrupted expansion in its history. And also like in Australia, there was no sign in December 2019 that the upswing was soon to end.[53]

One problem lingered. Even by the end of 2019, a decade after recovery from the deep recession of 2009 had begun, government debt remained at a high level in many advanced economies. Already very high in Japan, government debt had increased in Europe and the United States during and after the 2008 financial crisis. In the United States it had very nearly doubled to 100% of GDP by 2019. In Japan it was 200%.[54] Struggling with deep recessions, governments had spent big at a time when tax revenue was falling. The resulting deficits were financed by issuing bonds. It was usually the case that the more bonds governments offered, the higher the interest rates they would have to pay to persuade people to buy them. To offset this effect, the US Federal Reserve copied the policy the Bank of Japan (BoJ) had adopted a decade earlier, buying a large share of the additional bonds. A few years later, when Europe was hit by a debt crisis in Italy, Spain, Ireland and Portugal as well as slow growth in Germany and France, the European Central Bank (ECB) headed in the same direction. From three quarters of a trillion US dollars in treasury securities in 2010, the Federal Reserve had more than doubled its holdings by 2019.[55] The ECB and the BoJ had similarly increased their holdings of government bonds. The central banks' creation of additional money to buy the additional bonds should have caused inflation. But inflation did not pick up. On the contrary, it remained lower than the central banks wanted. By the end of 2019, not only Japan but also Europe and the United States had experienced a long period of high and rising government debt, very low interest rates and slow growth.

After the shock of the 2008 financial crisis, the Great Recession that followed, and a disappointingly slow recovery thereafter, the global economy was back on a track of modest employment and output growth. Yet the global growth slowdown looked likely to persist. Pondering the future growth of rich economies such as the United States, Europe, Japan, the United Kingdom and Canada, RBA economists published some of their conclusions in December 2019. They pointed out that growth in these economies, together accounting for about two fifths of world output, had been slowing for some time. It had been driven down by population ageing, slower investment growth and weaker productivity increases. The current and fairly slow growth rates of advanced economies were 'around potential'.[56] They were growing as fast as the growth of their labour force, capital stock and productivity permitted. One might conclude that, absent an increase in the rate of growth of output per hour worked, which there was no reason to expect, recent growth was as good as it would get, and probably better than it might be in the years to come, given the continuing decline in workforce growth.

The RBA economists also looked at China. The number of workers in China was then declining, and would continue to decline. Investment, they thought, had peaked as a share of output, and the additional output created by additional investment was anyway declining. As to productivity growth, that too had been falling for some years. If the recent trends in labour force and capital stock growth and productivity were extended out some years, China's growth would halve from just over 6% in 2019 to 3% or so by 2030.[57] In December 2019, the best informed projections pointed to a gradual slowing of world economic growth over the decades to come.

CHINA AND THE UNITED STATES

If a gradual slowdown in global growth was a long-term concern for Australia in 2019, a more immediate one was the threat to free trade and investment across national borders.

Over most of the years of accelerating economic globalisation — a time corresponding to Australia's long boom — China and the United States had pursued a mutually beneficial economic relationship. US President Richard Nixon and his National Security Advisor Henry Kissinger had opened political relations with China to encourage its break with the Soviet Union. The economic dimension was not a focus. When Kissinger made his secret visit to Beijing in 1971, China's economy was not much more than half the size of Australia's. It was another seven years before China began transforming collective farms into far more productive household plots, and opening up to the world in trade and investment. It was then another 20 years before China was able to join the WTO and Chinese-made manufacturing exports began to dominate global markets.

The economic relationship between the United States and China was often the ballast to their more difficult strategic relationship. American corporations invested in the vast China market. They used China's skilled and cheap labour to assemble products for the world market. China became the largest source of US imports, and the third biggest market for its exports.[58] As President George W Bush remarked when he agreed to terms for China's 2001 membership of the WTO, they were strategic competitors but, in economics, China and the United States could cooperate.[59]

Each became the other's largest trade partner, each had substantial investments in the other, each economy was transformed in ways influenced by the other. By 2019, each was far bigger than any other national economy except the other. Together they accounted for more than a third of global output and demand.

As China's economy advanced in size, range and complexity, however, and as large numbers of Americans became unhappy with their economic fortunes, the economic relationship between China and the United States came under strain. The United States complained that China exported too much and imported too little, that it ran up huge trade surpluses, heavily subsidised its export industries, stole intellectual property, and blocked foreign investment in many industries. Chinese imports had lacerated American manufacturing and destroyed American jobs.

Once insignificant, China's economy by the second decade of the twenty-first century was two thirds the size of America's and growing much faster. It was developing high technology industries such as solar panels and bullet trains, and planned more. At the same time, China's businesses were increasingly investing in companies abroad, becoming global corporations on the American and European model. The two great economies were in some respects becoming more alike than complementary.

For them, and for the rest of the world, this slow change presented two problems. If the United States and China were 'strategic competitors', as President Trump construed the relationship, should US security allies adopt the same attitude?[60] And, if China and the United States sought to form separate economic blocs, must US allies adhere to the US bloc? For countries such as Australia, Japan and South Korea — security allies of the United States and economic partners of China — that would be a problem.

Beginning in 2018, the Trump administration imposed higher and higher tariffs on a wider and wider range of imports from China. In response, China imposed counter-tariffs and cut back on soybean imports from the United States. The United States and China were in a trade war.

Yet, while expounded with conviction and prosecuted with vigour, by the time the Trump administration came to office in 2017 much of the US economic case against China was no longer true — if indeed it ever had been.

It was certainly true that the US goods trade deficit with China had more than quadrupled since 2001, the year China was admitted to the WTO with US support. But it was also true that over those years US exports to China had grown much faster than China's exports to the United States. The tariff cuts and other trade concessions China had made to win WTO entry worked in favour of the United States.[61]

And while China had indeed amassed large trade and current account surpluses in the first decade of the twenty-first century, by the end of the second decade they were largely gone.[62] By 2019, China's trade surplus with the rest of the world was just 1.25% of its GDP — far less, as a share of GDP, than the trade surpluses of Germany, Italy, Ireland or South Korea. Exports were over a third of China's GDP in 2006, and less than a fifth ten years later. When in 2010 future US Trade Representative Robert Lighthizer outlined to a congressional committee the aggressive tactics the United States should deploy to remedy the imbalance in trade with China,[63] China's trade surplus with the world was four times bigger as a share of China GDP, and its current account surplus nearly five times bigger than it would be when he began to execute the policy in 2017.

So too, in US manufacturing. There were 20 million jobs in US manufacturing in 1997. By 2010, when

Lighthizer spoke, there were 13 million left. But thereafter the trends changed. By 2016, manufacturing employment was back up to 15 million and continuing to increase.[64] What was true when the policy was framed in 2010 was no longer true when the Trump administration came to office.

Much of the discussion of the discord between China and the United States supposed that America was a declining power, soon to be overtaken by China as a rising power. In important respects these suppositions were wrong. The United States was not declining, and while China was certainly rising and was already the world's second biggest national economy, there was no assurance it could overtake the United States — or that it would much matter if it did.

Far from declining, up until the pandemic the US economy was doing well. Having recovered from the 2008 financial crisis, the United States had grown much faster than Japan or Germany, France or the United Kingdom over the last decade. It displayed remarkable ability to generate new products, new demands, new sources of profit and employment.

Comparisons using current market exchange rates showed China's GDP in 2019 was still only two thirds of America's GDP.[65] Measured using the World Bank's purchasing power parity (PPP) exchange rates, the positions reverse. US GDP was a little less than nine tenths of China's GDP.

Based on the relative purchasing power of currencies within their home country, PPP measures mainly reflect differences in labour costs. As China became richer, wages rose. Between 2008 and 2017, after-inflation wages rose 7% in the United States, but doubled in China. The difference between China's size measured in market exchange rates and the implied PPP exchange rate accordingly narrowed.[66]

In the IMF *World Economic Outlook* report of October 2017, China accounted for 17.7% of world economic output and the United States 15.5%, all in PPP terms.[67] But this PPP measure was based on the 2011 World Bank International Comparison Program (ICP). When in May 2020 the World Bank released its latest ICP results based on a 2017 survey, it showed that in 2017 the United States accounted for 16.3% of global output and China 16.4%.[68] In PPP terms, US output was $19.5 trillion and China's $19.6 trillion. The United States had caught up to China.

Whether China overtakes the United States in the next ten years (or ever) in market exchange rate terms depends to some extent on the exchange rate, but more fundamentally on how soon its output growth drops to the US rate. China has grown far more rapidly than the United States over many decades, but by 2019 was encountering a strong demographic headwind. The United States has a demographic advantage over most other advanced economies (but not Australia's). Its workforce will continue to increase, though more slowly. China's workforce, on the other hand, has already peaked and will decline over the next two decades.[69] To continue to outpace the United States, and to outpace it long enough to actually be a bigger economy in current exchange rate terms, it needs to beat US labour productivity growth handsomely.

It may well, but it is not certain. Japan, South Korea and Singapore, all of which saw very rapid growth as they caught up with the advanced economies, have now fallen to or below the rate of growth of the United States.[70] The more advanced China's economy becomes, the closer it gets to the global productivity frontier, the slower the productivity gains it is likely to make, and the more telling the decline in its workforce.

What was clear in 2019 was that in the next two decades, China and the United States would remain the two biggest national economies in the world, that they would be of roughly equivalent size, and that both would be technologically more advanced than they were in 2019. Since US defence spending was nearly three times China's, it was also likely that America would remain a far superior military power to China as long as it wished.[71]

By 2019 the US–China trade quarrel presented a serious threat to Australia. It also endangered the open trade and investment on which globalisation depends. Between its major security ally and its primary market, Australia was conflicted. When the Trump administration imposed higher tariffs on many imports from China and demanded changes in its foreign investment policies, China's neighbours were silent. Prime Minister Scott Morrison declared that Australia did not need to choose sides, and would not. The Trump administration declared China to be a 'strategic competitor'. Speaking in the United States, Prime Minister Morrison said that, for Australia, China was a 'strategic partner'.[72]

At the end of 2019, the United States and China declared a truce in their trade war. Following an agreement first announced on 13 December, China and the United States signed a 'first round' trade agreement on 15 January 2020. Under the deal, China would within two years lift its imports from the United States by $200 billion compared to the 2017 baseline.[73] Meanwhile, the United States kept penalty tariffs on $370 billion of imports from China. White House rhetoric had portended a US-initiated economic decoupling of China and America. The actual outcome was quite the reverse. It was, according to President Trump, 'the biggest deal anybody has ever seen'.[74] It committed China and the United States to more trade, not less. It was anything but a decoupling.

On the day of the White House signing ceremony, a traveller from Wuhan fell ill in Washington State and was admitted to hospital four days later. Tests showed the patient had the new virus, recently detected in China. The day before, the WHO tweeted that preliminary investigations by the Chinese authorities had found 'no clear evidence of human-to-human transmission'.[75] During a press briefing the same day, the WHO had also said of the 41 confirmed cases in the People's Republic of China (PRC) that 'it is certainly possible that there is limited human-to-human transmission'.[76]

Eight days later, China's government imposed a lockdown on the city of Wuhan to curb the spread of the new virus. At the end of the month, Trump declared a ban on arrivals of anyone who had been in China within the last two weeks, other than American citizens or resident aliens. The climax of two years of turbulent economic negotiations was a partial agreement on what seemed to be very strenuous targets, coming at roughly the same time as a pandemic that, within weeks of the agreement, raised the question of whether those targets were now impossible. Meanwhile, China and the United States would have a lot more than each other to worry about.

CHAPTER TWO

The pandemic

THE HUMAN COST

There was, we all remarked to each other through 2020, a feeling that 2019 was a very long time ago. COVID-19 had been so abrupt, it had for a while changed so much about our lives and in such unexpected and novel ways, that the world we had lived in a short while ago was suddenly distant, its unresolved struggles no longer pertinent. Sometimes we felt unmoored. We felt a need to remind ourselves why we were doing things in a certain way, why we hoped for certain things but not others, why we were as we were. We found ourselves questioning our assumptions. It was an illusion, a trick of the mind caused by the sudden cessation of routines we had accumulated over years, but it did free us a little to think freshly about our lives and the world in which we live them.

True in our own lives, it was also true in the public life of Australia. There too, the sudden cessation of well-established routines, and the sudden necessity to respond to circumstances very few people had experienced or even imagined, abruptly changed the nation's conduct.

Like war, the pandemic disarranged what was there, speeded up trends that might otherwise have evolved more slowly and terminated other trends once thought durable. It made intolerable the conduct that in easier times was merely incompetent. Some things important before the pandemic no longer mattered so much; other things were suddenly critical.

Things changed quickly. Some verities — the undesirability of budget deficits, for example — were no longer so. Behaviours once unimaginable became routine. It would have been difficult to believe in December 2019 that Australians could soon be ordered not to leave their own country or, if they had left, be prevented from returning until a room became available where they must spend 14 days in physical isolation (and soon, also, to pay for the room and meals). Difficult to believe that millions of people could be asked to work from home or that they would comply, or that this would prove not only feasible but possible to do with no great loss of output and so successfully that many would be reluctant to return to the old ways of catching a crowded bus or a train to an office in the city five days a week and staying there, eating a lunchtime sandwich at their desk, until it was time to catch a crowded bus or train back home. Reluctant, too, to get on a plane in the morning to fly to another city, take part in what during the pandemic came to be called 'face-to-face' to distinguish it from the multitude of other meetings now generically known as 'zooms', and to get in a car back to the airport for the trip home.

Difficult to believe, also, that the net debt of the Australian government, projected in December 2019 to reach zero in a decade, would within a few months be projected to instead more than double over the same decade. Difficult to believe that a new and highly infectious virus could first be detected in China and yet wreak far greater damage in America.

In the most ordinary aspects of life, small things changed. Some old social customs were suspended, some new ones introduced. Face-to-face meetings, handshakes and kisses went. Taxi drivers and Uber drivers asked passengers to sit in the back and wear masks. Golfers were warned not to touch flags or other people's clubs. If permitted to eat out, diners were obliged to register with the authorities. Masks became common, as did disinfectant sprays and the reminder to thoroughly wash one's hands. Zoom participants were offered a camera view of their colleagues' bedrooms and living rooms, the art on the walls, the books on the shelves. Participants experimented with different backdrops available on their software. They might be in front of the Parthenon, or on a beach. They might be anywhere in the world other than sitting in front of their laptop in the second bedroom of their home in Brunswick, Victoria.

It was not only appearances that changed. For more than a year, people talked about the pandemic as they had once discussed the weather. It was a shared experience, common to the whole species. Everywhere on the globe the symptoms and the course of the disease were the same, the measures to address it much the same. Everyone, everywhere, thought about masks, social distancing, washing hands, without distinction between rich countries and poor countries, the powerful and the powerless. Homeless people and national leaders could be and were infected by the same disease, displayed the same symptoms. The pandemic followed its own rules. The United States, spending more on health than any other country on earth,[77] had a death rate a hundred times higher than Mali, one of the poorest countries on the planet.[78]

So much was revealed, or created. For many years the economic region of East Asia had been growing faster than any other. Better prepared for a pandemic, more community-minded, with governments more vigorous in their response, East Asian nations experienced the pandemic earlier than the rest of the world and controlled it more effectively. The death rates were fractions of those in Europe, North America and South America. After the initial shock, their economic growth rates recovered more quickly. Once thought to be dependent on Europe and the United States, they again proved to be self-sustaining. In their handling of the pandemic and in their economic response, Australia and New Zealand followed the East Asian pattern. Australia's economic integration into the East Asian region — an economic community that counted China as its principal member — was affirmed.

The disease was so contagious that small mistakes could manifest in vast consequences. Incompetence was discerned. Whether the army, the police or security guards should control quarantine at city hotels in Melbourne could have been a decision of no great importance. It was the sort of decision that might never make it up to the top level. The people in quarantine were, after all, sensible law-abiding civilians. The job was to bring them meals, supervise their daily open-air exercise period, note their complaints and otherwise make sure they stayed in their rooms. The average bureaucrat might sensibly have decided it was not necessary to employ soldiers or police to guard compliant civilians in a hotel. It would smack of martial law. All was well until it became apparent that some private security guards had become infected and spread the disease in their home communities. The fallout from that small decision was thousands more infections, hundreds more deaths, a bigger economic loss than Victoria had suffered in the whole pandemic thereto, and a searching inquiry that for all its powers and intellectual force did not find it at all easy to identify exactly who authorised the action, or when, or why.

Or there was the decision to allow the release of passengers from the cruise ship *Ruby Princess* in Sydney. Again, it was taken well down the chain and based on what was later said to be an incorrect interpretation of the rules and insufficient information from the ship. A tiny and everyday decision leading to hundreds of infections, and avoidable deaths.

The most remarkable instance of the disease exponentially enlarging the consequence of ordinary mistakes was the electoral defeat of President Trump. That really did change the world. In December 2019, the polls were not so good for Donald Trump, but he had plenty of time to demolish his probable opponent, Joe Biden, in the presidential race. The economy, after all, was in good shape, with unemployment below 4% and every likelihood that America's longest expansion would continue through 2020. He was closing a big trade deal with China. In January 2020, the Trump campaign had plenty of money and was reportedly planning to focus on states that had marginally voted for Hillary Clinton, hoping to make them Republican gains in November. The pandemic destroyed his administration, which was shown to be incompetent, untruthful, uncaring. The president could have taken responsibility and led a national response to the virus, but he did not. He played down its dangers, made foolish claims. The baby boomer generation — the one threatened with death and among his most devoted supporters — peeled away. So did suburban white women. With new highs in infections recorded in the last weeks of the campaign, with potential vaccines still in the early testing stages, with every possibility the pandemic could get worse in America before it got better, the virus worked against Trump. On 3 November 2020, election day, the United States recorded 92 619 cases. Two days later, the number of cases reached 121 539 — a new daily record, though higher totals were to come. The number of infections per day in the United States was then more than four times higher than the entire number of infections in Australia since the pandemic began. Election day saw 6253 new infections in Wisconsin, 3664 in Michigan and 2868 in Pennsylvania — all states that voted for Trump in 2016 and flipped to Biden in 2020. By then the United States had recorded 9.7 million infections and the daily total was increasing. Nearly a quarter of a million Americans had died of the disease.[79] Without the pandemic, Trump stood a very good chance of winning a second term, as first term presidents almost always do. COVID-19 ran against him, and won.

The first Australian case was found in Melbourne on 25 January 2020 — a Chinese national who had arrived from Guangzhou a few days earlier. Later that same day, three other cases were reported in Australia. They had all been infected in Wuhan.

Through February the number of new cases in Australia steadily increased. It was not until 10 March that the cumulative number of cases passed 100, and by then public alarm had turned from bushfires to coronavirus. Now it was not long-stopped arrivals from China that accounted for new cases. It was often arrivals from the United

States, from cruise ships, from Europe. In the week following 10 March, the number of cases trebled to nearly 400. The week after, the number of cases increased fivefold. Told to stay home, to avoid non-essential travel, Australians remarked on the volume of bird song in the suddenly quiet cities. They became accustomed to new terms — social distancing, WFH, Zooming. They worried about whether to wear masks. They bought toilet paper in such vast quantities that the country ran out of it. We discussed epidemiology — a science that had not hitherto concerned many of us. There was kindness and fear. Travellers to the tiny coastal village in which I lived saw roughly lettered signs informing them that the road was closed.

With arriving foreign nationals required to quarantine, social distancing enforced, sporting venues, movie theatres, bars and restaurants closed, the number of new cases in this first wave of the virus peaked at close to 500 a day towards the end of March. Even so, by early April the coronavirus had killed more than 50 Australians and the cumulative number of cases was approaching 6000 and rising.

By June the pandemic appeared well contained. The number of new infections fell to nine or so a day. States began to open up. In early July, however, Victoria discovered infection was rampant, largely the result of security guards catching the disease and unknowingly spreading it to their communities. By the end of July, Australia was recording more than 700 cases a day, mostly in Melbourne. Even with increasingly stringent lockdown measures, it was not until October that the number of infections fell back to the daily numbers last seen in June.

By the end of 2020, there had been more than 28 000 cases in Australia, and over 900 deaths caused by the disease. Four fifths of the infections and nine tenths of the deaths were in Victoria.

Gradually the restrictions eased. By early 2021, vaccines were already being produced and administered, and interstate travel bans were being relaxed. Often there were zero new COVID-19 cases reported. Foreign travel was still difficult and there were few foreign tourists, but universities were hoping to enrol new foreign students for the 2021 academic year.

An island continent with an uncrowded population and good health services, Australia coped a lot better than the United Kingdom, the United States, Italy, France or Spain. Yet it had been the most astonishing and alarming public health episode in the experience of Australians then living.

*

Some countries did better in the pandemic than Australia; many did worse.

The course of the pandemic did not fit expectations. It was first identified in China, which was not surprising. That had been the case with some earlier viral infections. The subsequent spread defied prediction, however. Two months before the WHO announced the novel virus, a new Global Health Security Index ranked countries by their preparedness for a major disease outbreak. Published by a public health unit at Johns Hopkins University and *The Economist* Intelligence Unit, the index ranked the United States as the best prepared of the 195 nations surveyed.[80] Given that the United States spent 17% of GDP on health and was the biggest, richest and most advanced economy in the world, that ranking was as expected. The United Kingdom, with its widely admired National Health Service, was number two. China came in at 51 of the 195 surveyed. Mali was 147th.

The actual experience would be very different. What really mattered, the world discovered, was not advanced medical care, top quality hospitals or advanced science. What mattered was the quality of political leadership, prior experience of epidemics, community consent and compliance with unusual restrictions, mass testing, isolation of active cases, social distancing and, if necessary, lockdowns. What mattered in constraining infections and deaths were simple things, guided by public health science and effected promptly.

Though the disease had been first identified in China — and soon appeared in Japan, South Korea and Taiwan — China proved more adept at slowing the infection rate. Prepared by earlier epidemics, other East Asian nations responded rapidly.

By the beginning of 2021, the United States had registered over 20 million COVID-19 cases since the first infections had been reported a year earlier, and the trajectory was still rising. The death toll had passed 360 000 and continued to increase. By contrast, China, with four times the population, had reported under 5000 deaths, total. In China, the number of reported new cases per day by January 2021 was well under 100. In the United States, new record highs were reached, then exceeded. The number of deaths per hundred thousand Americans was more than 300 times that of the Chinese. Australia's death rate was one thirtieth of that in the United States. Even so, it was ten times the rate of China.

The United States had achieved some success in curbing infections after the sudden and vast increase in cases in New York, San Francisco and

Seattle in March, April and May. With summer and the easing of restrictions, there was a fresh and more terrible epidemic between the two coasts, soon of greater severity than the first shock. This time young people were more often infected. Partly because the victims were young, partly due to medical advances, and partly because more older people were now sufficiently concerned to adopt the recommended precautions of minimising contact and wearing masks, the death rate sharply declined.

Europeans watched the new wave of American infection with pity and horror until they discovered their infection rates, too, were rising dramatically as restrictions were lifted, intra-European travel resumed, and summer encouraged group events. By October, there were many more cases in Europe and the United States than during the worst of the first wave of the pandemic, and the infection rate in Europe and the United States (per million people) was roughly the same. Death rates were well down compared to the April peak, but the infection rate was so relentless that the United Kingdom and Europe had to shut down again.[81]

By January 2021, a little more than a year after the pandemic began, there had been over 90 million cases worldwide and 1.9 million deaths.[82] The United States still had many more cases than any other country, but by then Western Europe was well in front on infections per thousand people. There were still very serious epidemics in the United Kingdom, Argentina, Colombia, Nepal and Libya. Otherwise, the number of infections was declining. The developing world had done considerably better than the developed. Mali's rate was 1.49 per hundred thousand, and China's smaller still. India's was 11.1 per hundred thousand. Though it had four times the population of the United States, by the beginning of 2021, India had recorded only half the number of cases.

Controlling the pandemic had required shutting down industries that depended on physical contact, disrupting the usual pattern of transport, work, shopping, eating out and entertainment. It required sudden and vast redeployments of resources to testing, caring for the infected, and the acquisition of medical equipment and protective clothing. This displacement became apparent in the economic cost of the pandemic.

THE ECONOMIC IMPACT
Australia's economic output contracted a little in the first quarter of 2020, and a lot in the second quarter, quite enough to satisfy the usual definition of a recession. The long upswing that had changed Australia

was abruptly over. It had improbably continued through the 1997 Asian Financial Crisis, the 1998 Long Term Capital Management Crisis, the 2001 Tech Wreck in the United States and Europe, the 2008 GFC and, for that matter, the disappearance of Australia's own extraordinary mining investment boom, only to be terminated by an event that had not been included in any of the many grim prophesies of its inevitable end.

Australians had been warned that they were complacent, exhibiting an economic 'reform fatigue' that would inevitably destroy their prosperity. They were warned of a reckless accumulation of mortgage debt, lack of research and development spending, too much red tape, poor business management, inflexible industrial relations, high marginal tax rates on personal income, high taxation on profits, not enough tax on fresh food, a 'vertical fiscal imbalance' between state governments and the Australian government, woeful ignorance, lack of firm leadership, and so forth and so on. And not only those shortcomings, but also that the puzzlingly long upswing was an illusion because it all depended on a few thousand miners and their machines excavating iron ore to ship to China. It was a long list of failures, of reasons the upswing could not continue, of shortcomings that must be remedied by painful but necessary changes, a long list the upswing blithely survived and that never included a new virus first detected in Wuhan, China.

For that economic damage there was a mitigation of sorts already at hand. It would prove to be the economic equivalent of a vaccine but, unlike the long-awaited medical vaccine, it was immediately available.

On Saturday 5 January 2019, a year to the day before the WHO first posted details about a cluster of cases of 'pneumonia' of unknown cause on its globally accessible Event Information System, a speaker at the American Economic Association annual meeting in Atlanta offered what would become the intellectual underpinning of the global economic response to the pandemic.

In his presidential address, the eminent French–American economist Olivier Blanchard, a former IMF chief economist and a celebrated faculty member at MIT, reflected on the phenomenon of low interest rates on government bonds in many advanced economies. He reminded his audience of a simple and well-known fact obscured by fervent debates about government deficits, debt and central banks. This was that so long as the interest rate on government bonds was less than the growth rate of the economy, 'public debt may have no fiscal cost'.[83] Any specified level of debt would fall as a share of GDP over time because the growth rate of the debt was the bond rate, which was less than the growth rate of GDP. Of course, governments could choose to spend a lot more than their income, and so add to their debt compared to GDP. But the arithmetic was that so long as the deficit — the gap between spending and income — was no bigger than the interest payment on government debt, and so long as that interest rate was less than the growth of the economy, the ratio of debt to national income would either stay the same or fall. Assuming that taxes rose at the rate of growth of GDP, government revenue would always be growing faster than debt. As Blanchard pointed out, this largely explained the slow decline as a share of GDP of the immense debts the United States had accumulated during the Second World War.

It followed that if it became necessary to spend, governments should not be inhibited by the thought that it would be necessary to pay it back later. Even with a lot of spending in this generation, a later generation might well be faced with lower debt compared to GDP than the current generation. Like many really useful contributions to the economic policy debate, it was a very simple point, a reminder of what was well known, made at the right time. It did not require an economic model. Anyone could verify it with pencil and paper. But it would be of great consequence. It drew on a vast and well-known economic literature on debt sustainability. Most of that literature went to what government could not or should not do. Blanchard's contribution was to remind policymakers of what they could and should do. Favourably referenced by RBA Deputy Governor Guy Debelle in a speech on 30 June 2020, Blanchard's conclusions would reappear in the Australian government budget delivered on 6 October 2020.[84] The idea Blanchard expounded became the key to managing the economic impact of the pandemic in many advanced economies, and also the frame for its most enduring aftermath.

In its Treasury department, Australia had the good fortune to find a head who had long before thought through the economic problems presented by a pandemic. In a Treasury working paper published in February 2006, future Treasury Secretary Steven Kennedy and colleagues Jim Thomson and Petar Vujanovic looked at the economic effects of pandemics such as avian influenza and global flu. They concluded that a collapse in confidence and the withdrawal of labour were the two biggest unfavourable impacts. Accordingly, policies to promote a quick return to work and to restore confidence and consumption would be the 'most effective in offsetting the adverse economic consequences of a pandemic'.[85] Those policies would need funding, and on a scale Kennedy in 2006 could hardly have imagined he himself would propose in 2020.

The economic wreckage caused by coronavirus was abrupt, frightening and savage. Australia was on track to lose a tenth of its annual national production. Even with the Australian government spending hundreds of billions on employment and income support, even with the central bank taking interest rates to rock bottom and acquiring one way or another more than half of the additional debt the government issued to pay for its spending in the first six months of 2020, output fell by 7% in the three months to June compared to the previous quarter, and by 6.3% compared to the same quarter in 2019. Compared to the June quarter in 2019, the average real income of Australians had fallen 7.4%. By July, over a million Australians were unemployed.

Abrupt, savage, frightening — but also short and unexpectedly shallow. It was a deliberate recession, one brought about by government and by people's fear of infection. It was not widely noticed that through the four months of what was often thought to be a general economic collapse, important parts of the Australian economy kept working. Mining and farming continued. So did manufacturing and major construction work. Electricity, gas and water utilities stayed at work. Throughout Australia, public servants were still working, often at home. Tradespeople, cleaners, gardeners more often than not were working. Most health workers remained on the job, busier than ever. Schools and childcare facilities remained open in most places, continuing to employ their staff. Office workers found that new technologies enabled them to work as productively from home. Media staff struggled to keep up with the demand for news and entertainment. It may have been the case that many service workers who remained in jobs could not produce as much as before. Yet so long as they were paid, they could sustain their usual spending and were counted in Australia's total output. Though universities were closed, for example, university staff were paid, and university 'output' was as before. Soon, they were teaching online. All up, and notwithstanding that Australia was often reported to be in 'lockdown', most of the Australian workforce kept working, either from their usual place of work or from home.

The economic collapse, such as it was, centred in discretionary retail such as clothing and furniture, local and foreign travel, and sports, entertainment and the arts. The virus forced people out of shopping malls unless they had to buy food and groceries. Department stores David Jones and Myer temporarily closed their doors, as did fashion clothing retailers. Planes were grounded. Pubs, clubs and restaurants were closed. Any event likely to draw a crowd — a concert, a football game, a movie — was called off. When the numbers for the three months ending June 2020 were later published, they revealed that the big fall in GDP for that quarter was almost entirely caused by a fall in household consumption spending. There was a correspondingly huge increase in household savings. Due to government payments, income was actually up in the quarter.[86] The fall in consumption, and the corresponding fall in output in industries such as food services, medical services, transport, sports and recreation, administrative services and so forth was not the result of a financial crisis, a turn in the business cycle, the failure of an export market, or any of the usual causes of recession. It was due, as the Australian Bureau of Statistics remarked, to 'movement restrictions' in response to the pandemic.

An important characteristic of this kind of recession was that once the rate of new infection began to decline, the recession began to be over. There had been no destruction of physical capital, of offices or factories or machinery. There had been no loss of work skills. Technology and tastes had not changed. The headlines announcing plunging output and employment or collapsing retail sales — indicators that would in other years have alarmingly portrayed a sudden economic slump — did not carry the same message in this new circumstance. These numbers now meant that government edicts were being observed, that social distancing and partial lockdowns were working, that policies to slow or stop certain economic activities as likely to spread infection were effective.

The huge spending response by government, changes to the law to minimise bankruptcies, as well as timely and aggressive financial market support from the RBA, combined to minimise the financial dislocations and business failures usually revealed in sharp economic downturns.

Responding to the pandemic, the Australian government had announced in March 2020 a wage subsidy program expected to cost $130 billion. By late May, Treasury officials found that far fewer employers than expected were able to meet the criteria for business losses. The program cost was revised down by $60 billion, or about the same amount the Australian economy grew in each of recent years.

'Has the "lucky country" run out of luck?', the *Financial Times* headlined one story on Australia during the pandemic.[87] The fabled expansion was over. Yet compared to the countries to which it usually compared itself, Australia had a good pandemic. When the rich countries' international economic agency, the OECD, published its forecasts in June 2020, it expected Australia to experience a milder economic contraction over 2020 than any of the OECD's 37 members except South Korea. At 5%, the expected contraction in Australia would be less than half that forecast for the United Kingdom, a little over half of the expected contraction in the Euro zone, and less than the expected contraction in the United States, Germany and Canada.

When it met via video conference on 2 June 2020, the RBA board agreed, according to the minutes, it was 'possible that the downturn would be shallower than earlier expected'.[88] So it would be. When the RBA published a new set of forecasts on 6 November 2020, the expected peak unemployment rate was down to 8% in the fourth quarter, thence falling gradually to 6% two years later.[89]

The level of GDP at the end of 2021 would be about the same level as at the end of 2019. Soon enough that forecast too would prove pessimistic.

If it was a more cheerful scenario than the earlier forecasts, there was no doubt of the great economic cost of the pandemic. Even with good recovery, Australia would by the end of 2021 have lost perhaps 6% of GDP — the amount it may have risen over 2020 and 2021 without the pandemic. Measured as real GDP per head, living standards at the end of 2021 would still be below the level reached at the end of 2019. Employment would be considerably higher than it had been at the end of 2020, but probably still a little lower than it had been at the end of 2019. Unemployment at the end of 2021 could still be around 6.0% of the workforce, or more than 900 000 people. And by then, Australian government debt would be beyond what anyone could have imagined as the bushfires raged through south-eastern Australia two years earlier.

Corresponding to the comparative mildness of the pandemic in Australia, the economic damage would prove to be relatively light. Yet the full recovery of the Australian economy would depend also on the global economy, and many parts of it were in dire trouble. After a precipitous decline in the first three months of 2020, China had resumed production – though it was far from the level of output projected before coronavirus. Japan, South Korea, Taiwan and Singapore had also gone back to work, but with many areas of activity still disrupted and with intermittent episodes of reinfection. Spain, Italy and France had seen vertiginous drops in jobs and output and were only slowly returning to work. The east and west coasts of the United States, the location of much of its industry, were still grappling with the aftermath of an epidemic far more severe than China's.

Without much argument or political dispute, governments responded. In advanced economies the increase in government discretionary spending by October 2020 was just short of one tenth of GDP. The various forms of liquidity support — emergency loans, bank funding facilities and so forth — also totalled a tenth of GDP.[90] When Blanchard spoke in January 2019, US current government spending was one third of GDP. Less than 18 months later it had risen to over half of US GDP.[91] The US federal government deficit was a little under $1 trillion in 2019. In 2020, the Congressional Budget Office expected it would be three times higher, at more than $3 trillion.

*

Like the health impact, the economic impact of the pandemic was not as expected. The greatest damage was not in China where it had begun, or in the poor countries of Africa. It hit hard in the wealthy countries, and particularly in America, the United Kingdom and Western Europe — the areas where the health damage was also greatest. And as the IMF pointed out, the pattern of the slump was itself unusual. Recessions are usually apparent first and most dramatically in manufacturing. In this case, the downturn was most apparent and dramatic in anything that depended on the physical presence of people. Schools, colleges, shops, restaurants, movie theatres, concerts, sports events and tourism were hard hit, as were all activities requiring actual physical human contact. Construction, mining and manufacturing, by contrast, often stayed at work. After falling 16% between February and April 2020, US industrial production then rose by 15% from April to October.[92] After reaching an all-time high in late February 2020, the US S&P 500 stock index dramatically dropped one third by the end of March. With interest rates at record lows, confident the pandemic would one day end, exuberant investors then drove the index back up. By the end of November it was one tenth higher than its former record high of late February. An investor who bought in during the share price collapse of 2009 and hung on to the end of 2020 would have quadrupled her money, not counting dividends.

The most unexpected economic aspect of the pandemic was that while the damage was substantial, it was not as great or as enduring as first feared. In many wealthy countries, output collapsed in the second quarter of 2020, but was recovering by the third quarter. Income support sustained sales to households, often by package delivery. In the United States, retail sales from June 2020 were way above pre-pandemic levels despite new COVID-19 cases running at three times the level reached in April, when economic activity had plunged.[93] Even as Trump fell behind Biden in vote counting in the crucial state of Pennsylvania, the Bureau of Labor Statistics reported that the United States had added 638 000 jobs in October 2020, the sixth straight monthly gain. Of the 22 million jobs lost in March and April, half had been regained. Even so, US output in the fourth quarter of 2020 was expected to be markedly less than the fourth quarter of 2019. At 10.7 million, the number of workers without jobs in the United States in November 2020 was nearly double the total in February.

China quickly contained the virus with dramatic lockdowns. Output plummeted by nearly 7% in the first quarter of 2020 compared to the first quarter of 2019. By the second quarter, output was growing again, and that continued in the following quarters. Both exports and imports swiftly increased. China's economy, the IMF predicted in October 2020, would be one of the few to achieve growth over 2020 as a whole.[94] Its recovery was strong enough, warned the *Financial Times* in late November, to put at risk China's carbon reduction targets.[95] By the end of 2020 it was evident that, with a few exceptions, East Asia had handled the pandemic better than most other regions, and the economic growth gap between East Asia and the rest had widened. For Australia, with its exports predominantly to East Asia, that mattered. Despite the impact of travel bans on foreign students and tourists, Australian exports were less affected than earlier feared. By November 2020, goods exports were down just 4% on the level a year earlier.

By October, the IMF assessed that while the global economic impact had been very bad indeed, it was not as bad as earlier expected.[96] The forecasts, while still bleak, had also improved. The United States and Europe had been stronger than expected and global trade was recovering faster than expected, especially China's trade.[97]

Even so, on IMF projections, the difference between the increase in global output in 2019 and the fall in 2020 would be equivalent to a global loss of output of around US$6 trillion, or more than three times the total annual output of an economy the size of Australia's. Global trade was expected to fall 10% in 2020. Comparing the second quarter of 2020 to the fourth quarter of 2019, the International Labour Organization calculated that the world economy had lost the equivalent of 400 million full-time jobs, disproportionately among women, low wages earners and young people.

The cost to government budgets was also huge. In the fiscal year ending 30 September 2020, the US budget deficit tripled to $3.1 trillion — over 16% of GDP. Spending had increased 47% over the previous year. US federal government debt to GDP rose to over 100%, and kept going. The IMF expected 2020/21 budget deficits of one fifth of GDP in Canada and the United States, a twelfth in China, and a tenth in Australia.[98]

CHINA AND THE UNITED STATES

Caught unprepared by the pandemic, the Trump administration blamed China for causing it, for failing to notify the WHO in good time, and for underestimating the threat it presented. As the US death toll rose and Trump's re-election looked more difficult, his rhetoric blaming China became more strident. 'We must hold accountable the nation which unleashed this plague onto the world: China', he told the United Nations in late September, in a speech that had to be taped at the White House.[99]

America's restrictions on both the use of US technology by Chinese businesses and their access to the US market became more confining through the pandemic. Huawei's access to products that used US technologies was banned, no matter where those products were made or by whom. Under US pressure, Huawei was banned from the UK's 5G market, despite an earlier decision to permit use in some parts of the network. The Trump administration sought bans on both TikTok and WeChat, successful Chinese-owned apps. China had long banned Google, Facebook and WhatsApp, so its possibilities for direct retaliation were limited.

Yet, while Trump vocally blamed China for the pandemic and threatened it would 'pay a big price for what they've done to the world',[100] his administration did not resume the trade war with China during the pandemic.

And though there were plenty of examples of irritations in the economic and political relationship during the pandemic, they did not amount to a more general decoupling of the economies of the United States and China, or anything remotely resembling it. Nor were there signs that European or East Asian economies had begun decoupling from China, or intended to do so.

The trade dispute remained suspended. Committed to demanding targets for imports from America but beleaguered by the pandemic, China was running well behind its commitments through 2020. On the data to July 2020, China's imports of all goods covered by the January agreement were running at about half of those that would be required to meet the targets.[101] It had not broken the agreement, which did not set monthly targets, and US Trade Representative Robert Lighthizer did not publicly complain. Each month's shortfall, however, would have to be made up later, and the shortfalls were accumulating. The US trade deficit with China was falling, which was satisfactory to the Trump administration even if the overall trade deficit with the world was rising. But, even into 2021, it was by no means apparent that the results of the trade agreement would be good or bad for the relationship between the United States and China — especially since the new administration need not accept responsibility for the outcome.

There had not been a noticeable exodus of US investment in China.[102] Foreign direct investment overall into China in the first half of 2020 was down only 4% on the 2019 rate.[103] The comparable falls for Australia were 41%, and for the United States 61%. By October 2020, according to China's Ministry of Commerce, foreign direct investment had returned to the same level as a year earlier. To the annoyance of the Trump administration, Bloomberg reported that in 2020, Chinese corporations were on track to raise $9.1 billion from US financial markets — a higher total than any year since 2014.[104]

When the United States first imposed penalty tariffs on imports from China, it was widely reported that it had concentrated on high technology products, partly to inhibit China's technological development and particularly products that had a military application. As it happened, these were not US mass market products. Phones and computers — high technology products with a big market in the United States — were excluded from the penalty tariffs.

While additional and specific restrictions had been imposed on some high technology exports to China, trade between the two in these products remained strong.[105] Comparing the first seven months of 2020 to the first seven months of 2019, US exports of advanced technology products (ATPs) to China were down, with the difference due to the category including passenger planes and engines. China's exports of ATPs to the United States were also down, with the fall in the category including personal computers. Given the downturn in consumer spending due to the pandemic, the changes in ATPs did not look to be related to US restrictions on either exports or imports of the products.

As for US businesses in China, they seemed little affected by the trade quarrel. A US–China Chamber of Commerce survey early in the pandemic did not reveal any strong desire to quit China,[106] and US businesses complained less of issues such as unfair treatment or forced transfer of intellectual property that had earlier concerned them. The data is always a couple of years late, but US statistics show that sales by US majority-owned affiliates in China (including Hong Kong) were higher in 2018 than in 2017.[107]

In 2017 and 2018, the most prominent issues included China's demands that some US businesses wanting to operate in China would need to form joint ventures with Chinese businesses and transfer intellectual property into the new joint entity. The United States also sought fewer restrictions on US financial businesses entering the China market. Another issue was, of course, the trade deficit with China. One way or another, and with little acknowledgement, many of these issues were addressed and ameliorated, if not resolved, in the Trump administration before the pandemic, or during it.

CHAPTER THREE

After the pandemic

THE GLOBAL ECONOMY

Early or late, with more damage or less, most countries are through the worst of the pandemic. Our former lives are resuming. We are again getting up in the morning and going to work, buying groceries, eating out, attending games, concerts and ceremonies, wondering what comes next. Though even now there are dangers in mass travel, though there are still places it is unwise to visit, and crowds unsafe to join, output and employment are growing again. As early as the fourth quarter of 2020, nine months after the WHO had declared a pandemic and at a time when COVID-19 infections were still surging in Europe and America, output in most countries was on the way up. Vaccines were already available and being widely administered in the first quarter of 2021.

By January, the US S&P 500 share index was more than a tenth higher than its all-time high ten months earlier.

Many closed businesses will not reopen. Many workers laid off during the pandemic are feeling discouraged and may never return to the workforce. The immense output loss of the pandemic can never be recovered. After rebounding strongly in the early phase of the recovery, growth in output, incomes and jobs is slowing. Yet, over the next few years, over the next decade, the potential for global growth is much the same as expected before the pandemic. And while more people will work from home and more business meetings will be conducted online, and while the existing trend to shop online has been accelerated and deepened, the foundations of the global economy are unchanged.

Today's world economy is much like yesterday's. Offices, factories and farms are much the same as they were before the pandemic, people's skills are the same, technology is the same. Unlike many other economic contractions, this one was not caused by a major financial crisis, nor has it yet resulted in one. It was an administered economic contraction, the direct result of lockdowns, travel bans and social distancing.

Global growth over the next decade will be slower than before the pandemic, but that was already expected. The workforce in the major economies was already growing more slowly, or was already contracting. In China, Germany and Japan, the number of workers was already falling before the pandemic. In the United States and the United Kingdom, workforce growth is slowing. While the workforce is still growing in India, the Arab world and Sub-Saharan Africa, the economic weight of these countries is insufficient to make up for declines elsewhere.

For reasons not entirely clear, the growth of output per worker slowed in the rich economies after the 2008 GFC.[108] This is evident in most advanced economies, including Australia. It is also true in China. Recovery from the pandemic saw an increase in productivity in many economies, the usual result early in recoveries when employment lags output. But that productivity spurt is unlikely to continue without new technologies, or changes in the product mix that we cannot now foresee.

The post-pandemic global economy is similar to the pre-pandemic economy, but not identical. The global economy that was so congenial to Australia's prosperity over three decades is now less familiar, and less congenial. Some features evident before are now magnified. Government debt, already high as governments and central banks responded to the 2008 financial crisis and the slow recovery from it, has now increased to counter the pandemic. Interest rates, already low as central banks drove them down to stimulate demand after the GFC, are now even lower.

As a result of the pandemic, not only have government debt and deficits become much bigger, so have the matched purchases of government debt by central banks. In October 2020, the IMF expected government debt in advanced economies to rise from 105% of GDP in 2019 to 125% by end 2021. It might then begin to decline, but if inflation and output growth remain slow, it may well creep up, even if governments are able to reduce their deficits. Much of the additional government debt is held by central banks.[109]

Global inflation has meanwhile fallen because of excess inventories and higher unemployment resulting from the pandemic. Because of slow growth in output and prices, government tax revenue will increase only slowly even after the global economy returns to and begins to exceed the production levels of 2019. The result will be large and continuing government deficits, more debt and more upward pressure on interest rates that can be offset only if central banks continue to accumulate government debt. The pandemic has made permanent a policy combination intended to be temporary. For many years to come, Australia will be in a world not only of slowing growth but also of rising government debt matched by central bank purchases of government debt, of low interest rates, and low inflation.

It is a world in which the role of central banks has changed. Before the pandemic, most declared they were focused on controlling inflation. Today, most advanced-economy central banks have acquired an additional responsibility to bear down on the interest rate on government debt. Having acquired substantial government debt during the pandemic, they will likely have to keep what they have, and quite probably buy more.

Bearing down on inflation and bearing down on government bond rates are sometimes compatible objectives, but mostly not. If for any reason there is an inflationary surge, a central bank cannot resist an increase in bond rates unless it buys more bonds, adding to inflationary pressure by creating more money and lowering the cost of credit. As the IMF argued in October 2020, 'credibility can suffer where central banks are regarded as conducting monetary policy to keep government borrowing costs low rather than to ensure price stability'. In those contexts, it added, 'inflation expectations can increase very quickly once governments begin running large fiscal deficits'.[110]

Analogous circumstances following the build-up of government debt in the Second World War were handled with increasing financial regulation, including foreign exchange control. That system eventually collapsed both of its own weight and because of an inflation surge it was unable to control. Concerned by this risk, governments are likely to aim at gradually reducing their debt compared to the size of their economies, limiting the expansion of spending or the reduction of taxes, and circumscribing their political options.

Lingering high unemployment is the legacy with the highest social cost. So long as global output is below the level reached at the end of 2019, the number of workers required to produce it will also be below the number employed at the end of 2019. It may well be into 2022 before global output exceeds the level reached at the end of 2019. In the meantime, the workforce has increased in size as new young workers join it and people who were not in the workforce seek jobs to recover some of their pandemic losses. There may well also be a large increase in overall productivity as businesses use the opportunity to close down marginal operations, introduce new technologies and run their machines harder. A sharp increase in productivity was evident in 2020 and may continue for a while. That too would contribute to higher unemployment for some time.

Most advanced economies must now deal with the twin problems of unemployment and government debt. Policies to reduce debt will increase unemployment, and policies to reduce unemployment will increase debt. That is the central policy problem of the third decade of the twenty-first century. In each year, in each country, governments must make fine judgements to trade one of these goals off against the other.

AUSTRALIA

Australia's post-pandemic circumstances are in some respects typical of all countries recovering from the pandemic, and in some respects atypical.

The Australian economy is growing again. After output fell by 7% in the second quarter of 2020 compared to the previous quarter, it rose 3% in the third quarter. Output in that quarter was then only 4% lower than in the December quarter of 2019, before the pandemic. With a strong fourth quarter in 2020 and again in the first quarter of 2021, Australia might find that by mid-2021 output has returned to the pre-pandemic level. Yet almost a million people were out of work as the recovery gathered pace, and many of them will remain unemployed for a long time. With employment growing more slowly than output, it would likely be towards the end of 2021 before the number of jobs is back to where it was in December 2019 — a level of employment that still left 700 000 people or 5% of the workforce searching for jobs. Meanwhile, many new jobseekers will have joined the search for work.

In the first sustained fall in living standards most Australians have ever experienced, average real income per person will probably not regain the level of 2019 until 2022. After increasing rapidly since 1991, household wealth slipped in the first half of 2020 — though those losses have since been mostly recouped with resilient home prices and rebounding share prices.

Along with the bulge in unemployment, the biggest and most enduring change is the sudden, immense increase in government debt. After declining over the nine years to 2019, the Australian government budget deficit reached a new peacetime high unimaginable three months before it actually and indisputably happened. Australian government debt is now higher than it has ever been and, with continuing deficits, will increase for some considerable time to come. A good deal of that new government debt is held by the RBA — another unexpected change and one that poses problems for the Bank and for the coordination of monetary and fiscal policy in coming years.

By the 2020/21 budget, presented only nine months after the first cases of coronavirus had appeared in Australia, and at a time when new pandemic cases arising from community transmission had dropped to almost negligible numbers, it was evident that the fiscal effect would trouble governments for at least another decade.

At just under a tenth of GDP, the underlying budget deficit for the financial year 2020/21 was as a share of GDP more than double the deficit in 2009/10, incurred as Australia responded to the GFC. But while the post-GFC deficits had effectively reached zero nine years later, the deficits caused by the pandemic will go on and on. Ten years on, the budget will, on Treasury forecasts, still be in deficit of around 1.4% of GDP.[111] Before the pandemic, the 2030/31 fiscal balance had been projected as a surplus 2% of GDP. The difference of 3.4% of GDP captured the lingering impact of higher spending and lower revenue during the pandemic, and a lower starting point for subsequent GDP growth.[112]

In December 2019, Treasurer Josh Frydenberg had projected Commonwealth net debt to reach zero in 2030/31 — a pleasing forecast in a world of rising government debt.[113] By the December 2020 Mid-Year Economic and Fiscal Outlook, net Commonwealth debt was expected to be 38.3% of

GDP in 2030/31, or well over a trillion dollars. All up, the pandemic and its consequences would by 2030/31 have added more than half a trillion dollars to 2019/20 debt, or more than a trillion dollars compared to the pre-pandemic forecast.[114]

Long after the pandemic has become a distant memory, long after it is replaced in public concern by other and more urgent calamities, the consequences will still be apparent in debt, the cost of servicing debt and the constraints debt will place on government and central bank options.

Since the Hawke government of the 1980s (and implicitly, much earlier), there has been a declared budget rule that over a business cycle, the recurrent expenses of government will be met by recurrent revenue. Deficits encountered in contractions will be redeemed in expansions. As *The Sydney Morning Herald* economics editor Ross Gittins astutely points out, that rule has now been put aside.[115]

Now the deficits will be so huge, the path of the economy so uncertain and government bond interest rates so low, that another rule is needed. It is not so much a rule as a hope. It is based on Blanchard's simple point: so long as the economy is growing faster than the interest rates on sovereign bonds (and so long as the growth of spending is constrained), Commonwealth debt will gradually decline as a share of GDP. As the Treasurer explained, 'with historically low interest rates, it is not necessary to run budget surpluses to stabilise and reduce debt as a share of GDP — provided the economy is growing steadily'.[116]

A great deal will depend, as Blanchard explained in Atlanta, on the interest rate the Commonwealth pays on its debt, compared to the rate at which the economy grows. It will thus at least partly depend on the RBA. If it is willing to continue buying bonds, and to hold the bonds it already has, the government bond rate will be lower than it would otherwise be. Not so long ago, it was understood that the governor of the RBA would not criticise fiscal policy, and the Treasurer would not criticise monetary policy. They were different domains, with each responsible for one but not the other. The RBA now finds itself inextricably tangled in budget policy as well as monetary policy.

If all goes well, the additional debt can be managed over the decades to come. Because ultra-low interest rates are expected to continue well into the future, the net cost of Commonwealth debt as a share of GDP was projected in the October 2020 budget to decline slightly, even though the amount of debt was increasing. Nor will the interest cost be large. Even for 2020/21 it will be just 0.9% of

GDP, and by 2023/24 it will have fallen to 0.8% of GDP.

But that outcome, and the projection of a continuing fall over the coming decade of the cost of debt as a share of GDP, is perhaps a little misleading. Before the pandemic, the interest cost of Australian government debt was around 4%.[117] During the pandemic, the ten-year bond rate fell dramatically. This allows the government to refinance its earlier debt at much lower interest rates as it falls due, while also locking in a ten-year term at low rates for the bulge in new debt in the fiscal years 2019/20 to 2023/24. This is largely why Australian government net interest payments, both as a dollar amount and as a share of GDP, were *higher* in 2018/19 (when debt was much smaller) than they are expected to be in any of the four years from 2020/21 to 2023/24.[118]

Even if the government bond rate subsequently increases over this decade, as it almost certainly will, the Commonwealth borrowing cost will only be affected some time later. In Treasury projections, net interest payments decline as a share of GDP comparing 2020/21 to 2030/31, despite net debt rising by nearly 8% of GDP — and despite Treasury's projection that the bond rate will rise to 5% in the next decade. Because it ends in 2030/31, the Treasury projection of debt and its cost does not address the impact of gradually refinancing much higher debt during the next decade at an interest rate five times higher than the rate in this decade. The most constraining impact of the 2020 pandemic may not hit the Australian government for another ten years.

Timing the reduction of deficits and the control of debt will require good judgement. As articulated by the Treasurer, the Australian government will not try to stabilise the growth of debt until unemployment is comfortably under 6%.[119] Presented as a commitment to an expansionary fiscal policy during a period of recovery, the actual scenario offered by the Treasurer in the October 2020 budget was quite different. On RBA forecasts, unemployment does not fall to 6% until the end of 2022. Yet Treasury forecasts that the deficit will have been reduced from 9.9% of GDP in 2020/21 to 4% in 2022/23. Well before unemployment falls to 6%, the budget will have turned contractionary. It will continue to be contractionary, with the deficit projected to fall to 3% of GDP in 2023/24. That, at least, is the plan.

Treasury projects a relatively small increase in tax revenue over the four years from 2020/21 to 2023/24, the result of bringing forward personal income tax cuts and business investment write-offs. To reach the deficit target of 3% of GDP in 2023/24, spending will have to fall by 8% of GDP — a cut of a magnitude not attempted in the half century of data. Treasury's forecasts assume that the private economy would come back quickly enough and in a big enough way to replace the government stimulus being withdrawn.

It is true that net debt to GDP continues to increase over this period (peaking in 2023/24), but that is because the starting point deficit is so big, not because it is being reduced slowly. The Treasurer and Treasury have suggested policy may need to be adjusted, depending on the strength of the recovery. The projected settings underline just how much skilled judgement will be involved in fiscal policy over this decade.

The forecast of falling debt to GDP after 2023/24 depends on the government bond rate continuing to be below the rate of growth of the economy. It also requires close spending control. On the Treasurer's projections it would depend on the deficit — the gap between government spending and government revenue — falling over four years to 2023/24 by 6% of GDP.

Managing the increased debt will preoccupy Australian government for years to come. Yet at 38.3% of GDP in 2030/31, Commonwealth net debt would still be far less compared to the size of the economy than will be true of Japan, the United States, most of Western Europe and the United Kingdom.[120]

Much depends on how low government bond interest rates remain, and for how long. For rates to stay as low as they are, bond buyers must continue to accept a rate of return on government bonds well below expected inflation. They must accept that the value of the bonds they buy will, after inflation, probably fall over time and, in the meantime, the return on the bond will be below the rate of inflation and below what they might expect to receive on alternative assets like shares in companies or loans to businesses.

As more bonds are issued, the usual response is for interest rates on bonds to rise. If interest rates rise more than elsewhere or are higher than elsewhere for a security of equivalent rating, the Australian dollar would likely rise as offshore investors buy Australian bonds. To minimise this effect, the RBA has already found itself obliged to mimic the conduct of other central banks and itself buy Australian government bonds. By the end of 2020, the RBA had more than trebled its holdings of Australian dollar investments, mainly though not only in Australian government bonds held either outright or as security against loans, and doubled its balance sheet. The increase in Australian dollar investments held by the RBA was equivalent to more than half of the increase in Commonwealth bond issuance since the pandemic began.

To suppress the rise in bond rates that would otherwise occur, the RBA will need to hold a large amount of Australian government bonds for many, many years. To the extent it does so, it helps keep interest rates lower than they would otherwise be, reduces the net cost to the taxpayer of Commonwealth debt and restrains a rise in the Australian dollar. But to the same extent, it also makes the RBA a partner in government budget policy — a role it has been reluctant to assume — and loosens the restraints on government borrowing by making it cheaper and more predictable. It also exposes to the Australian public the fact that the dollars they exchange among themselves for payment of goods and services, the dollars in which they measure or hold their wealth, are in the end just computer entries the central bank has conjured out of nothing.

RBA policy will be constrained by pressure to keep interest rates low. At the same time, the Australian government will be constrained by debt. For several years, the Commonwealth will be intent on reducing deficits and therefore reducing the rate of accumulation of debt. For some years, the Commonwealth will take more out than it puts in, because only if tax revenue is increasing faster than government payments can the deficit be reduced. It will try to constrain spending. It will remain reluctant to lower tax thresholds or rates, because that will either slow progress towards budget balance or put more pressure on government to find cuts. Unless and until there is a general economic setback, fiscal policy will be contractionary for a decade and perhaps a lot longer.

The float of the Australian dollar in 1983 freed the RBA from the need to use all its tools to achieve an exchange rate target that was largely determined in Treasury. Henceforward, the Bank was able to use its influence over interest rates to manage the ups and downs of the Australian economy by targeting an inflation rate. Authority over economic management shifted from the Treasury in Canberra to the RBA in Martin Place. But with interest rates now at rock bottom and a commitment to keep them low for a long time, the Bank has lost a good deal of its room to move. Treasury, meanwhile, has again demonstrated the power of changes in spending and deficits to influence the economy, and promptly. Fiscal policy has returned to centre stage of economic management, empowering the Treasurer and Treasury to manage economic fluctuations and marginalising the central bank — at least for some time.[121]

The pandemic is changing the way we think about the central bank and the government, and also about our financial investments. The 'risk free asset' that played a large role in portfolio construction and financial asset pricing has lost much of its attraction and its usefulness as a pricing benchmark.

Before the pandemic, bonds would typically constitute up to two fifths of a 'balanced' portfolio of equities, bonds and cash owned by individuals or pension funds. They did not pay much before the pandemic, but bonds were nonetheless held for their safety and the 'balance' they brought to a balanced portfolio of financial assets.

When share markets plunge, investors often buy bonds as a safer option. The price of bonds rises accordingly, and the interest rate on the bond falls accordingly. The rise in the price of bonds to some extent offsets the fall in the price of shares. But when the interest rate is less than 1%, the balancing effect is minimal. Since bonds no longer balance movements in equities and pay a very poor return anyway, why hold them?

Faced with this situation, most funds have reduced their allocation to bonds, which reduces demand for bonds even as governments increase the supply. The result increases pressure on central banks to take up the slack.

THE UNITED STATES, CHINA AND AUSTRALIA
Both China and the United States — the two biggest national economies and the two great powers — have

emerged from the pandemic belittled. For control of the pandemic, no nation is indebted to the example of either. China handled the epidemic well, emerging with fewer deaths for its population size than most countries, including Australia. But China was also where the disease was first identified, and its closed authoritarian style allowed the virus' virulence to be underestimated for a few critical weeks at the end of 2019 and the beginning of 2020.

For its part, the Trump administration at first underestimated the impact of the virus and America's vulnerability, failed to prepare its stockpile of medical supplies or its hospitals, stumbled over red tape in producing testing kits, offered contradictory advice and poorly coordinated its governments and agencies. Despite having a more advanced medical system, despite its much greater wealth, despite having a population one quarter the size of China's, 75 times more Americans than Chinese were killed by the virus. There was nothing about America's example that stirred anything other than dread, pity and amazement in the rest of the world.

The prestige of both great national economies was tarnished by the pandemic. At the same time, the relatively more successful performance of the East Asia regional economy during the pandemic, the concurrent public exhibition of Australia's deteriorating relationship with China and the election of a new president in the United States all pointed to one central post-pandemic policy challenge. It was no longer only the quarrel between China and the United States that troubled Australia. It was now and more urgently the quarrel between Australia and China. Evidently annoyed by Australia's advocacy of an inquiry into the origins of the pandemic, by the end of 2020, China had imposed restrictions of one kind or another on Australian exports of beef, barley, wine, seafood, timber, coal and wheat.

Many Australian public commentators, myself included, know quite a lot about the United States and not much about China. We speak the same language as Americans. We are enthralled by their history and politics; we visit America with familiarity, ease and pleasure; we have American friends; we share a culture of political democracy, rule of law, market capitalism and high living standards. We read the same books, listen to the same music, watch the same movies, use the same social media, laugh at the same jokes. America is the most popular destination for Australians studying abroad. We esteem the good opinion of Americans and, in many professional fields, regard publication or recognition in the United States as superior to recognition at home. Our financial markets still follow America's, even if our economy no longer does. And while Australia's various national security arms will always declare their singular focus on Australian interests, the fact remains that most of the threat intelligence about the world beyond the South Pacific and most of Australia's military technology and a great deal of its military hardware comes from the United States. Australia hosts American military training camps and joint intelligence facilities. Australian military officers are embedded in US Indo–Pacific Command, and Australia sustains a large military delegation attached to its embassy in Washington. Australia's national security officials sometimes assimilate an American point of view.

By contrast, we visit China infrequently. Tourist travel is easy and interesting, but to visit professionally and safely, one needs a formal invitation, the correct visa, a schedule of people to meet. Contacts who are actually useful are prized beyond measure. Without fluent Mandarin, we rely on drivers or taxis rather than public transport to get about, we have few informal exchanges, and either meet only fluent English-speaking Chinese or do the best we can with translators. Compared to Washington, Beijing is a trying work place. I lived for ten years within fourteen blocks of the US Capitol and, at one time, planned on taking up US citizenship. I suppose

I have visited China no more than half a dozen times, and never for much more than a week.

Perhaps this is changing, and younger Australians are more open to a greater variety of cultural influences, without ranking America at the top. Perhaps, but for my generation it was inevitable and as it had to be. For Australians, America is and will remain a preeminent cultural centre of the world. Its literature, its political and economic thought, its ideals and values, augment us. It is true of both the left and the right of Australian political and cultural attitudes, not least because America does indeed contain multitudes. But because of the familiarity of the United States and relative unfamiliarity of China, many of us who find themselves thinking and writing about Australia in the world are consciously or unconsciously drawn to an American point of view. What is good for America, we presume, is good for Australia. We share this way of seeing the world with the British, though we have long lost the habit of seeing the world from a British point of view. This Australian rapport with America is foreign to the American way of seeing the world, which is from a decidedly American point of view.

Australia is not America, and it has different interests. Australia is not a great power. With its submarines, fighter-bombers, small but well-trained army, its reconnaissance and intelligence capabilities, its wealth in skills, communications and physical capital, its political unity, the obstacles presented by its surrounding seas and vast deserts, Australia has a formidable capacity to defend itself. Unless allied with a bigger power, however, it has little capacity to militarily intervene in other countries, other than some of the island nations of the South Pacific. The United States is a bigger military power than China. Australia is a much smaller power than either. Nor is Australia formally part of some larger regional group of nations with similar economies and shared security interests, like the European Union. It has a formal military alliance with the United States that would complicate the plans of any potential aggressor, but that — for all its elaboration — imposes no concrete obligation on the parties except to consult if either finds itself in a military conflict in the Pacific region.

There are other pertinent differences. Australia's total production is around one fiftieth of global production, its population less than one hundredth of global population. Compared to a state of the United States, it now has a bigger economy than Ohio, but a much smaller one than California, Texas, Florida or New York. The United States runs a substantial trade deficit with China, while Australia runs a substantial surplus. East Asia accounts for three quarters of Australian goods exports, but only a quarter of US goods exports.[122] Mexico and Canada are together a bigger export destination for the United States than all of East Asia. Together, China and Hong Kong account for less than one tenth of US goods exports. For Australia in 2020, they accounted for more than two fifths of goods exports.

Australia designs its trade policy structure around the objective of increasing integration into East Asia, a region dominated by China's economy. America does not. Its closest trade relations are with its neighbours, Canada and Mexico — neither of them important trade partners for Australia. Australia recognised the People's Republic of China in 1972, long after the United Kingdom but well before the United States. Even before recognition it traded with China, despite US disapproval.[123] Australia has a fairly comprehensive bilateral free trade agreement with China, one negotiated under both Labor and Liberal governments.[124] The United States does not. As a precondition for that agreement, Australia has long treated China as a 'market economy' — a long-standing Chinese global goal. America does not. During the pandemic, Australia signed the Regional Comprehensive Economic Partnership (RCEP), a trade agreement that includes China, the ASEAN states, South Korea, Japan and New Zealand. It does not include the United States. Australia is also a member of the Trans-Pacific Partnership (TPP) agreement, which will enhance economic integration of its members. The Trump administration withdrew from the negotiations for that agreement; China was not a party. Australia has a bilateral free trade agreement with the United States. In the 14 years between the agreement coming into force in 2005 and the eve of the pandemic, the value of goods exports to the United States increased by nearly 50% — a solid rise. Goods exports to China over the same period increased by over 800%.

None of these plain facts derogates from Australia's economic and social success. They remind us that Australia is not a great power. It cannot think of itself as China thinks of itself, and it has national interests that are different to those of China. So too, it cannot think of itself as America thinks of itself. It cannot adopt the stances that may be suitable for America, or the alliances or the enmities that may be suitable for America, because it is not America. It need not debate the best way to compete with other great powers because it is not a great power. It is not a strategic competitor of either China or America. It does not debate the best way to impose its values on the rest of the world, because it has no capacity to impose its values anyway. It may admire America, share its values, enjoy its culture, cultivate its goodwill; it may encourage America to act in a manner consistent with Australia's security; but Australia's national interests are not America's national interests.

The pandemic helped change the US administration, but in respect of China there is not a lot of difference between the declaratory attitude of the Trump administration towards China and the attitude of the Biden administration that replaced it. Republicans and Democrats both interpret China's growing weight as a challenge to American predominance. After four years of Trump, however, China and the United States have moved on. The trade agreement reached in 2019 imposes heavy obligations on China, which it is committed to meeting. During the Trump administration, China also moved ahead on intellectual property protection and foreign investment in financial services. Between the United States and China, trade and foreign investment issues may well move back to routine, negotiable disagreements.

The emphasis in the competition is changing. As *The Wall Street Journal* reported in November 2020, 'The American campaign to hinder Chinese technological advances has been among Washington's few bipartisan efforts of the past several years.'[125]

Biden came to office with the declared intent of using government to advance American superiority in education, research, science and frontier technology, and particularly in areas where China had caught up.[126] These areas include telecommunications and artificial intelligence. Concurrently, and responding to the Trump administration's policy of refusing US technologies to Chinese businesses, China has in its new five-year plan doubled down on state programs to develop its own advanced computer chips and other technologies in which the United States remains dominant. Expensive for both countries, for the rest of the world this kind of competition poses far fewer risks and promises greater benefits in technological advances than the trade war pursued in the Trump administration. Both the United States and China will be leaders in technology for decades to come. It follows that Australia and other third countries should decline to be channelled by one side into agreements that hinder access to the technologies of the other.

The Biden administration also came to office with an overt commitment to work with its allies to restrain China's industry subsidies. Australia, in contrast to the United States, Europe and China, has some but not many of these subsidies. It could usefully participate in any such negotiation, while recognising that the US Congress, the European

Commission and China will all be reluctant to limit their authority to extend subsidies not confined by existing WTO rules.

From the Australian point of view, the important thing is not whether the United States sees China as a strategic competitor — which to the United States it inevitably is — but how that competition is played and, in particular, the distinction between the economic realm and the security realm. If it attends to this distinction, the Biden administration has an opportunity to reset the US–China relationship in a way that recognises and responds to strategic competition between the two, but does not propose or encourage the separation of the global economy into China-led and US-led wings. Serious decoupling would not only pose impossible choices for Australia and other American allies, but also force China to assume an unwanted role as an economic adversary of the United States, an adversary compelled to create its own zone in the global economy.

It will be difficult for the United States and China to manage, but not impossible. The West and the Soviet Union were not only different in their political structures, but also in their economic organisation. China and the United States have different political structures, but much greater similarities in their economic organisation. A higher proportion of

Chinese people own their own homes than do Americans. Government spending in China is a markedly smaller share of its GDP than US government spending of US GDP.[127] Most of China's exports and most of its manufactures are produced by privately owned rather than state businesses. Most employees work for privately owned businesses. The governments of both countries extensively subsidise business with policy objectives in mind. In both, most business decisions are made on commercial grounds. In both, government works hand in glove with business to promote national economic success. The United States is a democracy and China is a one-party state; this aside, they can do business.

Australia's contemporary economic success, its success as a society and its power and place in the world have been built on economic globalisation. It has been built not only on its own increasing openness, but also on the increasing openness of other economies. It follows that anything that hinders economic globalisation, anything that tends to close what has opened, anything that divides the world into hostile blocs, is probably against Australia's national interests. Australia's future prosperity, its safety, will be enhanced if the global economy flourishes;

diminished if the global economy is degraded. So too, anything that hinders China's prosperity and its growth also hinders Australia's prosperity and growth, because Australia's economy is integrated with the regional economy of which China is the biggest part.

Pressed in November 2018 about the emerging US–China trade and technology conflict, Prime Minister Scott Morrison told reporters in Singapore that Australia did not have to choose between the two, and would not choose. He repeated the policy in his October 2019 Lowy Lecture. 'Even during an era of great power competition, Australia does not have to choose between the United States and China,' he said, adding that, for Australia, China is a comprehensive strategic partner and 'the strategic importance of our relationship is clear'.[128]

The truth is that Australia chose long ago, and is locked into its choices. It chose its region, including its largest member, China, as the economic community to which it inescapably belongs. It also long ago chose the United States as a defence ally to support Australia's territorial independence and freedom of action.

There is a good deal of tension between these two choices, but no possibility that either will change. Like many other enduring foreign policy problems, it cannot be resolved. It must instead be managed.

However, it can only be managed if the Australian government has a clear and united understanding of Australia's interests and capable people to execute policies consistent with that understanding.

Already selling all it can to Japan and South Korea, Australia would not find new markets for iron ore and coal to replace even a small percentage of what it now sells to China. Nor can it easily replace exports of wine, meat, dairy products and manufactures to China. The largest share of foreign tourists are from China, as is the largest share of foreign students. Without trade with China, Australia's living standards would be lower, its economy smaller and its capacity to pay for military defence reduced. It is difficult to imagine plausible circumstances in which an Australian government would voluntarily cut exports to China. Australia cannot and will not decouple from China's economy any more than Japan, South Korea, Taiwan or Southeast Asia could, wish to, or will. Indeed, America has not and probably will not decouple either — as evident in the economic agreement between the United States and China reached as the pandemic began.

On the contrary, the economic relationship between Australia and China will likely deepen in coming decades as the incomes of hundreds of millions of Chinese consumers reach advanced economy levels. Higher exports to China will be driven by China's increasing demand for a more varied and expensive diet, better health care services, competitive funds management, tourism, English language tertiary education, sports and entertainment, and offshore assets. Australia is well placed to compete in all these markets. Japan, South Korea, Taiwan and Singapore, too, will become more integrated in a regional economy with China at its core. Australia's stance towards the US–China competition must therefore be informed by a recognition that what injures China's prosperity also injures Australia's prosperity. China's economic decoupling from North America or Europe is not in Australia's interests.

Nor will Australia decouple from its security arrangements with America. The United States will remain the primary source of advanced military technology and security intelligence. And no hostile power can discount the possibility that the United States would come to Australia's military aid if required. The security arrangements Australia has with America are therefore sufficiently valuable that no Australian government would voluntarily deprecate them, let alone relinquish them.

The tension between these two pillars of Australia's engagement with the world will continue for decades to come. The centrality of these relationships makes it all the more important for Australia to conduct them carefully and cleverly, always guided by a notion of Australia's long-term interests. China's growing role on the world stage, its authoritarian government, its suppression of internal dissent, its territorial claims and defence build-up in the South China Sea, together with the deterioration of the relationship between the United States and China, make this tension difficult to manage.

Through 2020, Australia had its own trade and investment quarrel with China — one that had arisen from a deteriorating bilateral relationship over the last decade. High-level contact had been suspended for over three years, the Australian Embassy in Beijing found its access to even routine engagement with Chinese officials restricted, and trade disputes became more frequent.

Australia complained of restrictions or threatened restrictions on Australian exports of beef, barley, coal and wine. Interpreted in Australia as entirely unwarranted bullying, probably in response to Australia's call for an independent inquiry into the origins of COVID-19, the trade dispute has not been entirely one-sided. For its part, Australian businesses have been zealous in their pursuit of anti-dumping actions against Chinese imports. Of 39 anti-dumping cases under active investigation in Australia in November 2020, 21 were against China. Of 294 anti-dumping cases brought by competitors and concluded by the Australian Anti-Dumping Commission since 2012, 173 or well over half had been against China.[129]

And, while officials complained of an anti-dumping action by China against Australian wine in August 2020, Treasurer Josh Frydenberg reportedly refused a proposed takeover by a Chinese-owned corporation of a Japanese-owned dairy business in Australia — a decision that did not appear to conform to any known Australian foreign investment policy and that over-ruled the advice of the Foreign Investment Review Board.[130] The Chinese Foreign Ministry spokesman told reporters in November 2020 that more than a dozen Chinese investment projects in Australia had been rejected by the Australian government, including the refusal to allow Chinese companies to participate in the 5G network construction.

The Australia–China trade and investment dispute is plainly serious — one that threatens not just a market for barley, wine and beef, but more fundamentally the entire trajectory of Australian integration into East Asia.

Australia should certainly not recognise China's criticism of Australian media reporting on China, or accept China's inference that Australia has no right to comment on human rights in China. But Australian governments do need to detach themselves from an American point of view on China, and insist on their own. Australia's call for an independent inquiry into the origins of the pandemic, for example, was announced by the foreign minister casually on a television program. It clearly followed a US push for such an investigation and a discussion between the foreign minister and the US Secretary of State shortly before.[131] Determined not to take sides in the economic dispute between China and the United States, and to follow its own independent interests in its policy towards China, Australia needs to make a point not only of declaring so, but also of doing so.

Conclusion

IS GLOBALISATION DEAD?

Through 2020, the pandemic was frequently said to be reversing globalisation by stoking nationalist resentments, encouraging protectionism and discouraging cross-border trade and investment.[132] It is certainly true that countries closed their borders against foreigners and that various restrictions on cross-border trade in medical supplies were proposed and sometimes implemented. Yet it is also true that countries shared information about the virus and its spread, the WHO was able to coordinate and publicise high frequency data, and countries learned from each other about ways to control the virus and treat the victims. So too, the economic remedies have been broadly the same in most countries. It was a universal, shared experience. Like individuals, countries were both isolating and communicating. For a while, nations had more in common than they usually suppose. In these respects, the pandemic also underlined just how pervasive and irreversible economic globalisation has become.

Many countries imposed temporary restrictions on the export of what they deemed to be essential medical equipment in short supply, and many removed tariffs or other restrictions on the import of these supplies.[133] There was otherwise no evidence of a general or widespread increase in trade barriers during the pandemic.

The pandemic itself saw international trade falling, as might have been expected. In many economies, demand and production fell as a result of lockdowns or measures imposed to enforce social distancing. International and domestic travel was eliminated or cut back, discretionary retail selling collapsed, museums, cinemas and concert halls were closed. Global trade fell as a consequence of large parts of some economies stopping. But through the pandemic there was no state-sponsored interdiction of foreign trade, except in medical goods thought to be in short supply. Trade recovered further and faster than overall output. Even by August 2020, six months after the pandemic began, the WTO discerned some signs that the collapse of trade evident earlier may have bottomed out, a finding replicated in the trade monitor of the Netherlands Central Bank.[134] The November WTO Trade Barometer discerned a 'dramatic' improvement in world merchandise trade compared to earlier readings.

Many of the predictions of a sharp change to the nature or extent of globalisation are the same as those made before the pandemic, and have very little to do with the specific impact of it. They are complaints about 'unfair' trade by China, losses of manufacturing jobs in advanced economies, trade and technology competition between the United States and China, and the need for the United States and its allies to preserve a certain world order against China's ambition to impose a different one.

THE IDEA OF ORDER

It is widely said that the United States created a global economic order after the Second World War, which China is now trying to change. This global order, it is said, was responsible for the rapid rise in trade and investment that supported global prosperity and rising living standards including, from 1978 onwards, in China. Its earliest institutions were the IMF, the World Bank and the General Agreement on Tariffs and Trade (GATT). All grew out of the 1944 Bretton Woods conference of the wartime allies against Germany and Japan.

Yet this global economic order was never a single set of rules about economic organisation, and it was always changing anyway. Britain was the major partner of the United States in devising the new institutions. From mid-1945, Britain was led by a Labour government committed to the nationalisation of health services and key industries such as coal and steel. Negotiations for the United Kingdom were led by John Maynard Keynes, a formidable opponent of the US negotiator Harry Dexter White. The global order did not and could not authorise a single form of economic arrangements. Certainly, the Soviet Union and its satellites were excluded from the system — not because they were not capitalist market economies, but because they had become strategic adversaries of the United States.

The agreements at Bretton Woods and after replaced the pre-war gold standard for foreign exchange values with a US dollar fixed exchange rate standard backed by a US commitment to a gold standard for its currency. Twenty-five years later, the United States abandoned a fixed gold value for its currency, and the rest of the world soon abandoned exchange rates fixed on the US dollar. The IMF's role changed. The GATT became the WTO at the beginning of 1995, some months after completion of the last comprehensive global deal — the Uruguay

Round. It is now well over a quarter of a century since that global trade deal, and there is no sign another is likely. Most of what was thought to be the architecture of the global economy created after the Second World War no longer exists, or not in the form then created.

In this global economy, there is no central authority. There are no police to enforce rules. There are no enforceable decisions on international investment beyond those mechanisms mutually accepted by sovereign countries or commercial businesses.

And while there are a great many rulemaking or policymaking or dispute settling bodies to deal with cross-border issues of trade, investment, standards, corporate law, consumer protection, safety, communications, transport and so forth, and while it is also true that the United States is almost always a big player in these organisations, it is not true that the United States directs them.

There is a strong case to grant China the status, at the IMF and the World Bank, equivalent to its achievement as the world's first or second biggest economy. Yet while it is surely sensible to accord China the weight it deserves in these bodies, it will not create a new world order or significantly amend the existing order. The IMF is not a rulemaking institution. Nor is the World Bank or, for that matter, the Asian Development Bank (ADB), the China-chaired Asian Infrastructure Investment Bank (AIIB), or the OECD. All are useful institutions, all have a purpose in sustaining an international community. They are all institutions that Australia should and does support, and in which it competes for notice and influence. But they do not manage the global economy.

What does have a bearing is rules on trade. That is why the WTO is far more important to Australia's economic future. But the WTO is less important than it was. Not only is it more than a quarter of a century since its members concluded a global trade agreement, but regional trade agreements have now overtaken global agreements in encouraging cross-border trade. Under the Trump administration, the United States shut down the appellate mechanism of the WTO by blocking appointments to it. Without an operating appellate body, an appeal against a ruling by a WTO dispute settlement panel goes off into a void, leaving a plaintiff state without WTO authority to enact trade sanctions against a state that has violated the rules. In a demonstration of durability of arrangements that are in the mutual interest, the function of the appellate jurisdiction of the WTO has to some extent been replicated by a consortium of trading nations.[135] This consortium includes China, but not the United States.

Multinational institutions and the agreements that support them are important, but the foundation of the global economy, like that of a national economy, is actually the enforceability of contracts and logic of markets. There is no global authority to arbitrate or enforce contracts between the residents of one nation and another. National legal authorities may do so, or may recognise the authority of an international body to do so. Particular markets and industries may have model contracts and preferred means of resolving disputes. But there is no international authority to resolve commercial contract disputes or enforce judgements. Trade flourishes because abiding by rules is in everyone's interests. There is a framework of understandings, but trade between countries, like trade within countries, is largely governed by the market logic of prices, quantities, competitiveness, the quality of labour, capital, technology, the ambition of business entrepreneurs and so forth. It is not guaranteed by the United States.

RECONSTRUCTION

After the biggest global health shock in our lives, after the abrupt disappearance of an Australian prosperity so prolonged that, until recently, most of us living in Australia knew only routine increments to our getting and spending, we find ourselves drifting through the wreckage of our assumptions about ourselves and the world economy. So where are we, and where are we going? What kind of world are we in, and how will it evolve?

We could begin with what this new world is not. As damaging as it has been, the pandemic effects on the world economy are unlikely to persist. The wounds will heal. The immense loss of output has already occurred. The loss has been taken. It is already slipping into our past. The world is coming back to work. Unlike the 2008 GFC, there has been remarkably little large-scale financial failure despite the sharp loss of income and output in the first half of 2020. A full recovery of international travel depends on widespread inoculation with the vaccines now available. Yet, unlike war, there has been no destruction of buildings, machinery, mines and ports. Many lives have been lost, but the global workforce is mostly intact and there has been little loss of work skills. There is no good reason to think that the path of global growth will in a few years be different from the path that it might have taken if not for the pandemic.

Contrary to predictions made during the worst of the pandemic and, for that matter, for years before the pandemic, economic globalisation is not dead. Globalisation has proved robust to many setbacks.

It is true that exports as a share of world output peaked in 2008 and plunged in the global financial crisis of that year. For several years, exports grew more slowly than world GDP, supporting warnings that globalisation was in retreat. But in the three years to 2019, exports were again growing more rapidly than output and, by 2019, exports were much the same share of world output they had been in 2008.[136] Export growth began once again leading output growth at much the same time that Donald Trump became president and the United Kingdom decided to leave the European Union — two other events said to be reversing globalisation. The fast pace of trade growth continued through Trump's presidency and the Brexit negotiations. Six months into the pandemic, the increase in world trade was already running faster than the increase in global industrial production.[137]

While the pandemic necessitated restrictions on travelling from one country to another, and sometimes from one region of a country to another, it also reminded nations of their interdependence. It was a global experience, common in varying degrees to all countries and the whole species. A disease that probably originated in China caused hundreds of thousands of deaths in Europe and America. Measures that succeeded in curbing the pandemic in one country usually succeeded in others; policies that failed in one country usually failed elsewhere too. Once its rate of contagion and morbidity became apparent, data on the disease was widely shared in the global health community.

And despite the vast bond purchases by developed country central banks, and particularly by the US Federal Reserve, and those purchases being funded by creating money, it is not a world where rampant inflation is a serious threat. Unless and until demand for goods and services outruns the supply of them, a substantial rise in inflation is unlikely. The Bank of Japan has been creating money to buy bonds for decades, without seeing the increase in inflation that was the declared aim of the policy. In the decade before the pandemic, the US Federal Reserve had more than doubled its balance sheet, creating money and using it to buy US government bonds. Inflation was on average lower, much lower, after the financial crisis than it had been before it.[138]

It still has adherents, but the whole notion of a direct and necessary link between central bank money creation and consumer price inflation failed the test of empirical experience decades ago.[139]

Nor is the post-pandemic world one where broad economic decoupling between China and the United States, or between US allies and China, is gathering pace — or happening at all. On the contrary, both China's exports and imports grew rapidly in the second half of 2020. Its imports of US farm products hit new records. The level of China's exports in the first nine months of 2020 was much the same as the first nine months of 2019, despite the pandemic.[140]

Decoupling the US economy from China's economy was one of the aims of the Trump administration's trade fight with China, at least in the minds of some Washington policymakers. If it were ever a serious intention, it has not been successful. Over the two years of the celebrated conflict — 2018 and 2019 — no large American corporation announced it was ceasing production in China, or abandoning the China market. Nor did any large corporations from Europe or Japan. The offshoring of labour-intensive production from China to Vietnam, Bangladesh and other countries with cheaper labour continued, as it had for years. Over the period, foreign investment in China increased — a result inconsistent with the notion that the rest of the world was decoupling from China.

Decoupling China from the world economy is evidently hard to do. One reason is that China's domestic market is now the second biggest national consumer market in the world, and every year the volume of demand increases more than in any other national market. General Motors sells more cars in China than in the United States; Apple sells more phones.[141] After the pandemic, as before it, this is not a market that US corporations will willingly abandon to their foreign competitors.

The pandemic has not toppled the 'international order' said to underpin global trade and investment. The defeat of Donald Trump has certainly brought the United States back as a more cooperative leader in forming global alliances and contributing to global rulemaking. But, like a national market economy, the global economy largely runs itself. It runs, as economies do, on countless billions of decisions by households and businesses responding to preferences, prices and profits. It is secured by contracts and understandings to which governments are not often a party, and by a commercial regulatory framework that may be more rigorously enforced in some countries than others but is broadly similar in most successful economies.

Nor has the experience of the pandemic revealed that the prosperity of the pre-pandemic Australian economy was an illusion. The long upswing ended, but not because of any fault inherent in Australia's economic structure or policies, or global economic circumstances. It ended essentially because a sharp downturn in output was a necessary condition for suppressing the pandemic. The expansion has now resumed.

Our new world is mostly the old world, with some important differences.[142] Much of the fall in the global production of goods and services, and most of the damage it caused, is in the past. But there are some lingering effects from the loss of income and output. It is still apparent in increased household and business indebtedness and, above all, in higher unemployment.

Global government indebtedness is another lingering result of the pandemic. This is the result of the spending undertaken to support incomes at a time when government revenue was falling. It is much higher in the advanced economies and especially in the United States, Japan, the United Kingdom and the European Union.[143] The rich economies were more easily able to borrow and typically have far bigger social support systems than poor and middle income countries. So long as sovereign interest rates stay low and nominal GDP growth remains markedly higher than the sovereign rate, the debt is manageable. But it will constrain governments' ability to handle new fiscal problems such as US social security funding, infrastructure building and jobs programs.

The experience of the pandemic emphatically underlined the superior economic performance of East Asia. After a sharp fall in the first quarter, China's economy actually expanded over 2020 as a whole, compared to 2019. South Korea, Taiwan and Japan all suppressed the infection earlier than Europe or America, and their economies rebounded more strongly. Southeast Asian economies were more uneven, but the output loss was small and the rebound faster and stronger than that expected in North America or Europe.

In the unhappy aftermath of economic calamities, people want to know who and what to blame. For the economic distress of the pandemic, there is nothing and no one to blame. It was not the result of poor leadership, of a regulatory oversight, bad business decisions, a policy mistake by a central bank, or even of what were once said to be the inevitable ups and downs of the business cycle. It was not inherent in Australia's long upswing that it would come to grief. The vast loss of income, output and jobs, the immense increase in government debt, was not caused by any economic fault that should now be corrected.

The economic distress was the necessary consequence of curbing infection. No nation found a way of suppressing the virus without suppressing economic activity. If they chose not to suppress the infection early, they paid later.

This peculiarity of the economic catastrophe of 2020 suggests Australia's immediate ambition should be to recover what it had in December 2019. Australians want the incomes they had then, the jobs they had then, the expectation of improving prosperity they had then. They want a world that is as congenial to their interests as it was then.

Some of this ambition is attainable. Restrictions are light and, to the extent they ever left it, Australians have returned to work. Output is recovering back to its 2019 level and through 2021 may well exceed it. Compared to the worst of the pandemic, there have already been big gains in jobs and hours worked. Migration, international tourism and the inflow of foreign students cannot be fully restored until vaccines are widely available, but the recovery of Australia's international trade in goods has encountered few impediments.

Even with a firm recovery in output, however, unemployment will remain high. To bring it down, governments need to sustain spending. Yet government debt is already very high. That is a central problem for government over the next few years — bringing unemployment down, within the constraint of rising debt.

Meanwhile, some problems apparent before the pandemic are now more troubling. The most important of these is the threat to the global economy presented by the competition between the United States and China, and Australia's own deteriorating trade relationship with China.

There is an agenda here of serious purpose and great national responsibility, a graver, heavier responsibility than Australia has had to meet for many decades. It demands thoughtful advice and skilful implementation from the public service and other institutions, and wise decisions from government. The reconstruction of Australia after the pandemic depends on their success.

Endnotes

1   Bush and grass fires scorched 5.3 million hectares of land in New South Wales (NSW) alone, blackening an area that accounts for more than 6% of the state. Within the south-eastern states, fire destroyed a total of 2439 homes and claimed 25 lives, including three NSW Rural Fire Service (RFS) volunteers and three US firefighters. These numbers were unrivalled in the state's history.

2   Bernard Lagan, 'Bushfires: Ash from Australia Threatens NZ Glaciers', *The Australian*, 8 December 2019, https://www.theaustralian.com.au/world/the-times/bushfires-ash-from-australia-threatens-nz-glaciers/news-story/cc78bf59db528b33865a7eea740a3541.

3   World Health Organization, 'Timeline of WHO's Response to COVID-19', *World Health Organization News*, 9 September 2020, https://www.who.int/news/item/29-06-2020-covidtimeline. It had been reported that China advised the WHO of the new virus on 31 December. According to the WHO timeline, that was the day WHO's Country Office in the People's Republic of China (PRC) picked up a media statement by the Wuhan Municipal Health Commission from their website on cases of 'viral pneumonia' in Wuhan. China responded to WHO queries on 3 January 2020.

4   Australian Bureau of Statistics, *ABS 3101.0 Australian Demographic Statistics, June 2019*, 19 December 2019, https://www.abs.gov.au/AUSSTATS/abs@.nsf/DetailsPage/3101.0Jun%202019?OpenDocument.

5   World Bank, *GDP Per Capita (Constant 2010 US$) — Australia, United States*, https://data.worldbank.org/indicator/NY.GDP.PCAP.KD?locations=AU-US.

6   Australian Bureau of Statistics, *ABS 6416.0 Residential Property Price Indexes: Eight Capital Cities*, June 2020, https://www.abs.gov.au/statistics/economy/price-indexes-and-inflation/residential-property-price-indexes-eight-capital-cities/latest-release.

7   From just over $200 billion in 1991 to $2.8 trillion dollars in December 2019.

8   Australian Bureau of Statistics, *ABS 6523.0 Household Income and Wealth, Australia 2017–18*, 12 July 2019, https://www.abs.gov.au/statistics/economy/finance/household-income-and-wealth-australia/latest-release.

9   The long post-war boom in Australia, for example, was replicated in most advanced economies at the time and, like them, ended in the early 1970s with dramatic increases in oil prices, rising wages and inflation, and central banks' responses to them. The deep Australian recession of 1980/81 again coincided with a US downturn, brought about by an ultimately successful decision by the US Federal Reserve to crush inflation. The subsequent upswing in Australia later in the 1980s ended with the recession of 1990/91, again coinciding with a downturn in the United States. In both countries, the recession was caused or amplified by financial deregulation. In the United States, it was reckless lending by newly deregulated savings and loan businesses; in Australia, by reckless property lending by the big four (and newly deregulated) Australian banks.

10 Coal exports, for example, doubled over the long boom but even so accounted for less than a thirtieth of nominal GDP in 2019.

11 Though manufacturing output had increased, it had declined from one tenth to one twentieth as a share of Australian output. Mining's share had increased by the share manufacturing had fallen, from just over one twentieth of output in 1991 to just under a tenth in 2019.

12 As measured by the ABS in the gap between hours worked and quality adjusted hours worked.

13 Australian Bureau of Statistics, *ABS 3412.0 Migration, Australia 2018–19*, 28 April 2020, https://www.abs.gov. au/statistics/people/population/migration-australia/latest-release.

14 Australian Bureau of Statistics, *ABS 6523.0 Household Income and Wealth, Australia 2017–18*, 12 July 2020, https://www.abs.gov.au/statistics/economy/finance/ household-income-and-wealth-australia/latest-release.

15 OECD, *Income Inequality*, https://data.oecd.org/inequality/ income-inequality.htm.

16 Australian Bureau of Statistics, *ABS 6523.0 Household Income and Wealth, Australia 2017–18*, 12 July 2020, https://www.abs.gov.au/statistics/economy/finance/ household-income-and-wealth-australia/latest-release.

17 In the United States, the share was 79.5%, the Netherlands 68.3%, Denmark 64%, Germany 59.8%, France 50.6% and New Zealand 52.9%. As with income, the United States is the outlier. On these numbers, the top 1% of US households commanded 42.5% of household wealth — nearly double the next highest (The Netherlands 27.8%, Austria 25.5%, Germany 23.7% and Denmark 23.6%) and not quite three times the Australian rate of 15%.

See OECD Statistics and Data Directorate, *Inequalities in Household Wealth across OECD Countries: Evidence from the OECD Wealth Distribution Database*, OECD Working Paper, 20 June 2018, https://www.oecd.org/officialdocuments/publicdisplaydocumentpdf/?cote=SDD/DOC(2018)1&docLanguage=En.

18   That was the slowest growth of per capita incomes over a ten-year period in Australia for at least half a century (except for the ten years to 2017/18, which was marginally lower at 9.4%).

19   In the ten years to 2018/19, output expanded by nearly 30%. It was slower than the 37% by which output expanded in the ten years to 2008/9. The peak was the ten years to 1971/72, when growth was 75%.

20   Simon Benson, 'Scott Morrison's Post-Pandemic Powerplay', *The Australian*, 18 May 2020, https://www.theaustralian.com.au/nation/morrison-pushes-for-new-order/news-story/152d2adb2d8e26e5f46d84ab9e4fb2ee.

21   Reserve Bank of Australia, *Household Sector — Household Wealth and Liabilities*, 4 November 2020, https://www.rba.gov.au/chart-pack/household-sector.html.

22   While household debt had reached 187% of household disposable income by March 2020, the required interest payment on that debt was 8% of disposable income — well below the peak of 13.3% reached in 2008. This amount was no higher than the share of interest in disposable income reached 18 years earlier, when household debt to disposable income was not quite two thirds of the share it had reached by the end of 2020.

23   Australian Treasury, *Mid-Year Economic and Fiscal Outlook 2019–20: December 2019*, Table E4, 323, https://budget.gov.au/2019-20/content/myefo/download/MYEFO_2019-20.pdf.

24   As RBA economist Gianna La Cava pointed out in March
     2019, some of the income attributed to profit is the rental
     value imputed to owner-occupied homes. When that is put
     aside, the labour share rises, though the decline in its share
     is still evident. The profit share also includes income to small
     and micro businesses, the owners of which often apportion
     as profit what is actually attributable to their own labour.
     However, the big influence is the mining sector. Most of the
     factor income in mining is attributable to profit, whereas
     in the economy as a whole, more than half is attributable
     to wages. Mining is highly capital intensive, and its high
     profit share is the payment for that capital. When mining
     surges as a share of GDP, as it has in recent years, the profit
     share surges. See Gianni La Cava, 'The Labour and Capital
     Shares of Income in Australia', *Reserve Bank of Australia
     Bulletin — March 2019*, 21 March 2019, https://www.
     rba.gov.au/publications/bulletin/2019/mar/the-labour-and-
     capital-shares-of-income-in-australia.html.

25   Productivity Commission, *PC Productivity Insights —
     Recent Productivity Trends*, No 1/2020, February 2020,
     5, https://www.pc.gov.au/research/ongoing/productivity-
     insights/recent-productivity-trends/productivity-insights-
     2020-productivity-trends.pdf.

26   Adam S Posen and Jeromin Zettelmeyer (eds), *Facing
     Up to Low Productivity Growth*, Peterson Institute
     for International Economics, (Washington: Columbia
     University Press, 2019).

27   Ibid, 15.

28   Though lower as a share of GDP than ten years earlier,
     research and development spending as a share of GDP in
     2019 was nonetheless markedly higher than it had been
     in most of the first decade of the twenty-first century,
     when productivity growth was higher. See OECD, *Gross
     Domestic Spending on R&D*, 2020, https://data.oecd.org/
     rd/gross-domestic-spending-on-r-d.htm.

29 Productivity Commission, 'Where to Next' in *Productivity Commission Insights*, No 3/2020, 40, https://www.pc.gov.au/research/ongoing/productivity-insights/long-term/productivity-insights-2020-long-term.docx.

30 Reserve Bank of Australia, *Minutes of the Monetary Policy Meeting of the Reserve Bank Board*, 3 December 2019, https://www.rba.gov.au/monetary-policy/rba-board-minutes/2019/2019-12-03.html.

31 Australian Treasury, *Mid-Year Economic and Fiscal Outlook 2019–20: December 2019*, https://budget.gov.au/2019-20/content/myefo/download/MYEFO_2019-20.pdf.

32 See Parliamentary Budget Office, *2020–21 Budget Snapshot*, 7 October 2020, https://www.aph.gov.au/About_Parliament/Parliamentary_Departments/Parliamentary_Budget_Office/Publications/Chart_packs/2020-21_Budget_Snapshot.

33 World Health Organization, 'Timeline of WHO's Response to COVID-19', *World Health Organization News*, 9 September 2020, https://www.who.int/news/item/29-06-2020-covidtimeline.

34 The WHO statement stated: 'Symptom onset of the 41 confirmed nCoV cases ranges from 8 December 2019 to 2 January 2020. No additional cases have been detected since 3 January 2020', https://www.who.int/csr/don/12-january-2020-novel-coronavirus-china/en/.

35 Federal Reserve Bank of St Louis, *Inflation, Consumer Prices for the United States*, 3 March 2020, https://fred.stlouisfed.org/series/FPCPITOTLZGUSA.

36 Unnoticed in 1979, but also premonitory, a report to the US Department of Energy concluded that carbon dioxide levels in the atmosphere would double as early as 2035, and no later than 2060, increasing global temperatures by 2 to 3 degrees Celsius. See Michelle Nijhuis, 'Early Warnings', *The New York Review of Books*, 27 June 2019,

https://www.nybooks.com/articles/2019/06/27/losing-earth-climate-early-warnings.

37 World Bank, *Regional Trade Agreements*, 5 April 2018, https://www.worldbank.org/en/topic/regional-integration/brief/regional-trade-agreements.

38 World Bank, *Exports of Goods and Services (% of GDP)*, https://data.worldbank.org/indicator/NE.EXP.GNFS.ZS.

39 Measured in constant 2010 US$. See World Bank, *GDP per Capita (Constant 2010 US$)*, https://data.worldbank.org/indicator/NY.GDP.PCAP.KD.

40 Ibid.

41 World Bank, *Exports of Goods and Services (% of GDP) — Australia*, https://data.worldbank.org/indicator/NE.EXP.GNFS.ZS?locations=AU.

42 The increase was from 57% to 76%. See World Integrated Trade Solution (WITS), *Trade Summary Database*, World Bank, https://wits.worldbank.org/#.

43 World Bank, *GDP (Current US$) — China, Australia, Japan*, https://data.worldbank.org/indicator/NY.GDP.MKTP.CD?locations=CN-AU-JP.

44 Calculated as the increase in the value of goods exports to China divided by the increase in nominal GDP over the 29 years to and including 2019.

45 The interregional trade share was 57.5% in 2018 — the latest estimate. The Asian Development Bank's 'Asia' includes South Asia and Central Asia as well as East Asia and the Pacific. See Asian Development Bank, *Asian Economic Integration Report 2019/2020: Demographic Change, Productivity, and the Role of Technology*, November 2019, https://www.adb.org/sites/default/files/publication/536691/aeir-2019-2020.pdf.

46 See the Reserve Bank of Australia's October 1991
    Bulletin on 'Financial Markets and the Economy in the
    September Quarter', https://www.rba.gov.au/publications/
    bulletin/1991/oct/1.html. Its commentary on the
    international economy covered the United States, Japan
    and Germany, but not China. Six years later, when the
    RBA issued its first *Statement on Monetary Policy* (SMP),
    the international economy assessment was still about
    the United States, Japan and Europe. South Korea had a
    paragraph, but China was fleetingly included in 'other Asia'.
    See Reserve Bank of Australia, *Semi-Annual Statement on
    Monetary Policy*, November 1997, https://www.rba.gov.
    au/publications/bulletin/1997/nov/2.html. Even a decade
    later, in the November 2007 SMP, commentary on China
    was minimal. See Reserve Bank of Australia, *Statement on
    Monetary Policy*, 12 November 2007, https://www.rba.gov.
    au/publications/smp/2007/nov/pdf/1107.pdf.

47 World Bank, *Exports of Goods and Services (% of GDP)*,
    https://data.worldbank.org/indicator/NE.EXP.GNFS.
    ZS?end=2008&start=1970.

48 After rising to 5.3% of world GDP in 2007 from less than
    1% 15 years earlier, foreign direct investment inflows
    had fallen to 1.6% in 2019. See World Bank, *Foreign
    Direct Investment, Net Inflows (% of GDP)*, https://data.
    worldbank.org/indicator/BX.KLT.DINV.WD.GD.ZS.

49 World Bank, *GDP Growth (Annual %) — OECD
    Member, United States*, https://data.worldbank.org/
    indicator/NY.GDP.MKTP.KD.ZG?locations=OE-US.

50 Organisation for Economic Co-operation and Development
    (OECD), *GDP per Hour Worked*, https://data.oecd.org/
    lprdty/gdp-per-hour-worked.htm.

51 World Bank, *GDP (Constant 2010 US$) — China*,
    https://data.worldbank.org/indicator/NY.GDP.MKTP.
    KD?locations=CN.

52   Dmitriy Plekhanov, 'Is China's Era of Cheap Labor Really Over?', *The Diplomat*, 13 December 2017, https://thediplomat.com/2017/12/is-chinas-era-of-cheap-labor-really-over. See also Steve Johnson, 'Offshoring Slows as Wages Rise in Some Emerging Economies', *Financial Times*, 19 December 2019, https://www.ft.com/content/258213ac-181c-11ea-b869-0971bffac109.

53   Jon Hilsenrath, 'The Verdict on Trump's Economic Stewardship, Before Covid and After', *The Wall Street Journal*, 14 October 2020, https://www.wsj.com/articles/trumps-economic-record-is-divided-before-covid-and-after-11602684180.

54   World Bank, *Central Government Debt, Total (% of GDP) — France, Germany, Japan, United States, OECD Members*, https://data.worldbank.org/indicator/GC.DOD.TOTL.GD.ZS?locations=FR-DE-JP-US-OE.

55   Federal Reserve Bank of St Louis, *Assets: Securities Held Outright: US Treasury Securities: All: Wednesday Level*, 25 November 2020, https://fred.stlouisfed.org/series/TREAST.

56   Reserve Bank of Australia, 'Potential Growth in Advanced Economies', *Reserve Bank of Australia Bulletin: December 2019*, 57, https://www.rba.gov.au/publications/bulletin/2019/dec/pdf/bulletin-2019-12.pdf.

57   Ivan Roberts and Brendan Russell 'Long-term Growth in China', *Reserve Bank of Australia Bulletin: December 2019*, 36, https://www.rba.gov.au/publications/bulletin/2019/dec/pdf/bulletin-2019-12.pdf.

58   United States Census Bureau, *Top Trading Partners — 2020*, https://www.census.gov/foreign-trade/statistics/highlights/toppartners.html.

59   'In Bush's Words: "Join Together in Making China a Normal Trading Partner"', *The New York Times*, 18 May 2000, https://www.nytimes.com/2000/05/18/world/in-

bush-s-words-join-together-in-making-china-a-normal-trading-partner.html.

60 Viewing China as a strategic competitor rather than a strategic partner was staple rhetoric of Republicans long before the Trump administration. For example, as a candidate for president, George W Bush used the distinction in August 1999. China, he said, should be viewed as a 'strategic competitor', not a 'strategic partner'. See Thomas W Lippman, 'The Tables Turn as a Bush Criticizes Clinton's Policy toward China', *The Washington Post*, 20 August 1999, https://www.washingtonpost.com/archive/politics/1999/08/20/the-tables-turn-as-a-bush-criticizes-clintons-policy-toward-china/4f9f7aad-ca6d-49ea-9838-9fc02d8541fe/.

61 United States Census Bureau, *Trade in Goods with China*, https://www.census.gov/foreign-trade/balance/c5700.html. From 2000 to 2016 China's goods exports to the United States increased by four and half times. US goods exports to China increased by seven times.

62 In 2007 its trade surplus peaked at 8.6% of China's GDP. By 2016 it was down to 2.3%, and heading lower. The current account surplus had similarly declined, from 10% in 2007 to 1.8% in 2016. See World Bank, *External Balance on Goods and Services (% of GDP)*, https://data.worldbank.org/indicator/NE.RSB.GNFS.ZS; and World Bank, *Net Trade in Goods and Services (BoP, Current US$)*, https://data.worldbank.org/indicator/BN.GSR.GNFS.CD.

63 Robert E Lighthizer, 'Testimony before the US–China Economic and Security Review Commission: Evaluating China's Role in the World Trade Organization over the Past Decade', US–China Economic and Security Review, 9 June 2010, https://www.uscc.gov/sites/default/files/6.9.10Lighthizer.pdf.

64 From 2000 to 2009 manufacturing as a share of GDP contracted from over 15% to under 12%. As a share of GDP, manufacturing was much the same in 2016 as in 2009, and as an absolute amount markedly higher. See Statista, *Number of Private Sector Manufacturing Employees in the United States from 1985 to 2019*, https://www.statista.com/statistics/664993/private-sector-manufacturing-employment-in-the-us/.

65 World Bank, *GDP (Current US$) — China, United States*, https://data.worldbank.org/indicator/NY.GDP.MKTP.CD?locations=CN-US.

66 While the average foreign exchange market value of the yuan was unchanged between 2015 and 2020, the calculated PPP value of the yuan depreciated as wages and incomes in China rose. The result was that the difference in size between the GDP of the United States and China measured in PPP narrowed.

67 International Monetary Fund, 'Table A. Classification by *World Economic Outlook* Groups and Their Shares in Aggregate GDP, Exports of Goods and Services, and Population, 2017', *World Economic Outlook: Seeking Sustainable Growth*, October 2017, 221, https://www.imf.org/~/media/Files/Publications/WEO/2017/October/pdf/main-chapter/text.ashx.

68 World Bank, 'Figure 1.2 PPP-Based GDP and Share of Global PPP-Based GDP, by Economy, 2017', *Purchasing Power Parities and the Size of World Economies*, 2017, 3, https://openknowledge.worldbank.org/bitstream/handle/10986/33623/9781464815300.pdf.

69 J Stewart Black and Allen J Morrison, 'Can China Avoid a Growth Crisis?', *Harvard Business Review*, Sept–Oct 2019, https://hbr.org/2019/09/can-china-avoid-a-growth-crisis.

70 International Monetary Fund, *Real GDP Growth — Annual Percentage Change Map*, 2020, IMF DataMapper, https://www.imf.org/external/datamapper/NGDP_RPCH@WEO/OEMDC/ADVEC/WEOWORLD.

71 Stockholm International Peace Research Institute, 'World Military Spending by Region, 1998–2019', *Military Expenditure*, https://www.sipri.org/research/armament-and-disarmament/arms-and-military-expenditure/military-expenditure.

72 Dennis Shanahan, 'Morrison Navigates between the US, China', *The Australian*, 21 September 2019, https://www.theaustralian.com.au/inquirer/morrison-navigates-between-the-us-china/news-story/44240183b2d34a28b0d488e73d6035be.

73 John Edwards, 'The US is Elbowing Australia and Allies in a Race for the China Market', *The Interpreter*, 28 January 2020, https://www.lowyinstitute.org/the-interpreter/us-elbowing-australia-and-allies-race-china-market. See also Ana Swanson and Alan Rappeport, 'Trump Signs China Trade Deal, Putting Economic Conflict on Pause', *The New York Times*, 15 January 2020, https://www.nytimes.com/2020/01/15/business/economy/china-trade-deal.html.

74 Dominic Rushe, 'Trump Signs China Trade Pact and Boasts of "The Biggest Deal Ever Seen"', *The Guardian*, 16 January 2020, https://www.theguardian.com/business/2020/jan/15/us-china-trade-deal-donald-trump. See also Linda Qiu, 'Trump Falsely Calls China Trade Agreement "Biggest Deal There Is"', *The New York Times*, 15 January 2020, https://www.nytimes.com/2020/01/15/us/politics/trump-china-trade-deal-fact-check.html.

75 Twitter, World Health Organization (WHO) Twitter Account, 14 January 2020, https://twitter.com/who/status/1217043229427761152?lang=en.

76 World Health Organization, 'Timeline of WHO's Response to COVID-19', *World Health Organization News*, 9 September 2020, https://www.who.int/news/item/29-06-2020-covidtimeline.

77 In 2019 the United States spent 17% of GDP on health. These figures assume that non-OECD countries spend less as a share of GDP than OECD countries. See OECD, *Health Expenditure and Financing*, https://stats.oecd.org/Index.aspx?DataSetCode=SHA.

78 As at October 2020. See Johns Hopkins Coronavirus Resource Center, https://coronavirus.jhu.edu/data/mortality.

79 'Covid in the US: Latest Map and Case Count', *The New York Times*, https://www.nytimes.com/interactive/2020/us/coronavirus-us-cases.html, accessed 3 November 2020.

80 'GHS Index: Global Health Security Index', Johns Hopkins, Bloomberg School of Public Health and *The Economist* Intelligence Unit, October 2019, https://www.ghsindex.org/wp-content/uploads/2019/10/2019-Global-Health-Security-Index.pdf. See also 'No Country Fully Prepared for Major Disease Outbreak, New Global Health Security Index Shows', Kaiser Family Foundation (KFF), 25 October 2019, https://www.kff.org/news-summary/no-country-fully-prepared-for-major-disease-outbreak-new-global-health-security-index-shows/.

81 See European Centre for Disease Prevention and Control, *Weekly Surveillance Report on COVID-19*, https://www.ecdc.europa.eu/en/covid-19/surveillance/weekly-surveillance-report, accessed 15 October 2020. See also Jason Douglas, Stacy Meichtry and Andrew Barnett, 'Europe Overtakes US in New Cases of Covid-19', *The Wall Street Journal*, 14 October 2020, https://www.wsj.com/articles/europe-overtakes-u-s-in-new-cases-of-covid-as-restrictions-tighten-11602669748.

82 'Covid World Map: Tracking the Global
    Outbreak', *The New York Times*, https://www.
    nytimes.com/interactive/2020/world/coronavirus-
    maps.html?action=click&module=Top%20
    Stories&pgtype=Homepage, accessed 9 January 2021.

83 Olivier J Blanchard, 'Public Debt and Low Interest Rates',
    Peterson Institute for International Economics, Working
    Paper No 19–4, 4 February 2019, https://papers.ssrn.com/
    sol3/papers.cfm?abstract_id=3346535#:~:text=Put%20
    bluntly%2C%20public%20debt%20may,rate%20of%20
    return%20on%20capital.

84 There were many complications to the story. For example,
    government spending could be wasteful and unnecessary
    and at the expense of spending that was useful. It was
    possible for government borrowing to be at the expense of
    private borrowing and investment, which could be more
    productive.

85 Steven Kennedy, Jim Thomson and Petar Vujanovic, '2006-
    01: A Primer on the Macroeconomic Effects of an Influenza
    Pandemic', The Australian Treasury, 15 February 2006,
    https://treasury.gov.au/publication/2006-01-a-primer-on-the-
    macroeconomic-effects-of-an-influenza-pandemic.

86 Australian Bureau of Statistics, *A Series of Unprecedented
    Events — The June Quarter 2020*, https://www.abs.gov.au/
    articles/series-unprecedented-events-june-quarter-2020.

87 Jamie Smyth, 'Australia: Has the "Lucky Country"
    Run Out of Luck?', *Financial Times*, 24 May 2020,
    https://www.ft.com/content/73c4f0b6-d5c7-47c8-b91c-
    8e84343dfd85.

88 Reserve Bank of Australia, *Minutes of the Monetary
    Policy Meeting of the Reserve Bank Board*, 2 June 2020,
    https://www.rba.gov.au/monetary-policy/rba-board-
    minutes/2020/2020-06-02.html.

89 Output through the year to the fourth quarter would fall 4%. By the fourth quarter of 2021 it would be 5% higher than the fourth quarter of 2020. Reserve Bank of Australia, *Forecast Table — November 2020 — 'Baseline' Scenario*, https://www.rba.gov.au/publications/smp/2020/nov/forecasts.html.

90 International Monetary Fund, *World Economic Outlook, Oct 2020: A Long and Difficult Ascent*, IMF, October 2020, 15/16, https://www.imf.org/-/media/Files/Publications/WEO/2020/October/English/text.ashx.

91 Federal Reserve Bank of St Louis, *Government Current Expenditures/Gross Domestic Product*, https://fred.stlouisfed.org/graph/?g=8fX.

92 Federal Reserve Bank of St Louis, *Industrial Production: Total Index*, https://fred.stlouisfed.org/series/INDPRO.

93 Federal Reserve Bank of St Louis, *Retailers Sales*, https://fred.stlouisfed.org/series/RETAILSMSA.

94 International Monetary Fund, *World Economic Outlook, Oct 2020: A Long and Difficult Ascent*, IMF, October 2020, https://www.imf.org/-/media/Files/Publications/WEO/2020/October/English/text.ashx.

95 Christian Shepherd and Thomas Hale, 'China's Economic Recovery Jeopardises Xi's Climate Pledge', *Financial Times*, 20 November 2020, https://www.ft.com/content/d452aef8-9fd7-422a-a034-4558f0e66e53.

96 International Monetary Fund, *World Economic Outlook, Oct 2020: A Long and Difficult Ascent*, IMF, October 2020, https://www.imf.org/-/media/Files/Publications/WEO/2020/October/English/text.ashx.

97 Global trade fell sharply in the early stages of the pandemic, for example, but even by October 2020 the IMF was expecting a reasonable recovery. Global trade

was expected to fall 10% in 2020, rising 8% in 2021 and settling to an increase of 4% in the medium term — a little faster than global GDP growth, though not much. The predictions were supported by rising trade in the second half of 2020.

98 International Monetary Fund, *Fiscal Monitor: Policies for the Recovery*, October 2020, 4, https://www.imf.org/-/media/Files/Publications/fiscal-monitor/2020/October/English/text.ashx.

99 The White House, 'Remarks by President Trump to the 75th Session of the United Nations General Assembly', 22 September 2020, https://www.whitehouse.gov/briefings-statements/remarks-president-trump-75th-session-united-nations-general-assembly/. It was notable, though, that while complaining of China's tardiness in notifying the world of the new disease, the Trump administration had proved reluctant to seek from the states rules on temporary lockdowns, social distancing, wearing masks, rapid testing and so forth, which worked elsewhere, even long after the high infection and morbidity rates of the disease became startlingly apparent.

100 James Griffiths, 'Trump Threatens China with Big Price "For What They've Done to the World" as Campaign Looks to Shift Blame', CNN, 8 October 2020, https://edition.cnn.com/2020/10/08/asia/trump-pence-china-debate-covid-intl-hnk/index.html.

101 Chad P Bown, 'US–China Phase One Tracker: China's Purchases of US Goods, as of October 2020', Peterson Institute for International Economics, 25 November 2020, https://www.piie.com/research/piie-charts/us-china-phase-one-tracker-chinas-purchases-us-goods.

102 Nicholas R Lardy, 'Despite the Rhetoric, US–China Financial Decoupling is Not Happening', Peterson Institute for International Economics, 2 July 2020,

https://www.piie.com/blogs/china-economic-watch/despite-rhetoric-us-china-financial-decoupling-not-happening

103 United Nations, '2020 H1 FDI Down 49%', *Investment Trends Monitor*, United Nations Conference on Trade and Development (UNCTAD), 27 October 2020, https://unctad.org/system/files/official-document/diaeiainf2020d4_en.pdf.

104 According to data compiled by Bloomberg, 'China-based companies have raised $9.1 billion by listing on US markets this year … putting 2020 on course for the highest annual total since 2014.' See Jeremy Goldkorn, 'Editor's Note for Monday, 2 November 2020', *SupChina*, 2 November 2020, https://supchina.com/2020/11/02/editors-note-for-monday-november-2-2020/.

105 United States Census Bureau, *US Trade with China in Advanced Technology Products — Monthly and Cumulative Data (in Millions US$)*, https://www.census.gov/foreign-trade/statistics/product/atp/2020/07/ctryatp/atp5700.html.

106 AmCham China, 'Supply Chain Challenges for US Companies in China', AmCham China and AmCham Shanghai, 17 April 2020, https://www.amchamchina.org/about/press-center/amcham-statement/supply-chain-challenges-for-us-companies-in-china.

107 Bureau of Economic Analysis, US Department of Commerce, *Activities of US Multinational Enterprises, 2018*, 21 August 2020, https://www.bea.gov/news/2020/activities-us-multinational-enterprises-2018.

108 World Bank, *GDP per Person Employed (Constant 2017 PPP $) — China*, https://data.worldbank.org/indicator/SL.GDP.PCAP.EM.KD?locations=CN.

109 Once thought of as generally feckless and ill-disciplined in fiscal matters, less developed economies have held to a more conservative path — not least because of the higher interest rates, and less appetite from lenders. Their sovereign debt to GDP was expected to rise from 55% of GDP to 65% — around half the GDP share in advanced economies.

110 International Monetary Fund, *World Economic Outlook, Oct 2020: A Long and Difficult Ascent*, IMF, October 2020, https://www.imf.org/-/media/Files/Publications/WEO/2020/October/English/text.ashx.

111 Australian Treasury, *Mid-Year Economic and Fiscal Outlook 2020–21, December 2020*, https://budget.gov.au/2020-21/content/myefo/download/myefo-2020-21.pdf.

112 See Parliamentary Budget Office, *2020–21 Budget Snapshot*, 7 October 2020, https://www.aph.gov.au/-/media/05_About_Parliament/54_Parliamentary_Depts/548_Parliamentary_Budget_Office/Reports/2020-21/Budget_snapshot/2020-21_Budget_Snapshot_PDF.PDF?la=en&hash=2EF42FA6A8C9E51F3C82C56D9F85143843DC3257.

113 Ibid.

114 In these projections, at 40% of GDP debt in 2030/31 would actually be less as a share of GDP than it would be earlier, in the middle of the decade. This is because the annual deficits as a share of GDP from the middle of the decade would be less than the projected rate of growth of the economy, or nominal GDP.

115 Ross Gittins, 'We're Edging towards a Big Change in How the Economy is Managed', *The Sydney Morning Herald*, 29 August 2020, https://www.smh.com.au/business/the-economy/we-re-edging-towards-a-big-change-in-how-the-economy-is-managed-20200828-p55q3i.html.

116 Treasurer Josh Frydenberg, 'Speech to the Australian Chamber of Commerce and Industry, Canberra', 24 September 2020, https://ministers.treasury.gov.au/ministers/josh-frydenberg-2018/speeches/speech-australian-chamber-commerce-and-industry-canberra.

117 Commonwealth of Australia, Statement 11: Historical Australian Government Data, Australian Budget 2020–21, https://budget.gov.au/2020-21/content/bp1/download/bp1_bs11_w.pdf.

118 The inclusion of Future Fund earnings in the net outcome probably accounts for some of the fall in net interest, but by no means all. See Commonwealth of Australia, Budget Paper No 1, Statement 11, Table 4, https://budget.gov.au/2020-21/content/bp1/download/bp1_bs11_w.pdf.

119 Phillip Coorey, 'No Budget Deficit Repair Until Jobless Below 6pc: Frydenberg', *Australian Financial Review*, 24 September 2020, https://www.afr.com/politics/federal/smaller-economy-will-prolong-deficits-frydenberg-20200923-p55yl8. See also Treasurer Josh Frydenberg, 'Budget Speech 2020–21', 6 October 2020, https://ministers.treasury.gov.au/ministers/josh-frydenberg-2018/speeches/budget-speech-2020-21.

120 International Monetary Fund, *Fiscal Monitor: Policies for the Recovery*, October 2020, https://www.imf.org/-/media/Files/Publications/fiscal-monitor/2020/October/English/text.ashx.

121 See speech by Treasury Secretary Steven Kennedy, 'Policy and the Evolution of Uncertainty', 5 November 2020, https://treasury.gov.au/speech/policy-and-evolution-uncertainty. See also James Glynn, 'Australian Treasury Expects Bigger Role for Fiscal Policy to Last', *The Wall Street Journal*, 5 November 2020, https://www.wsj.com/articles/australian-treasury-expects-bigger-role-for-fiscal-policy-to-last-11604553012.

122 United States Census Bureau, *Exhibit 14. US Trade in Goods by Selected Countries and Areas: 2020*, https://www.census.gov/foreign-trade/Press-Release/current_press_release/exh14.pdf.

123 For example, 'Australia became the largest source of China's western wheat imports in the first half of the 1960s despite the disapproval of the United States.' See David Lee, 'Our Trade with China Flourished Despite the Cold War', ADFA News, Canberra, 19 November 2020, https://www.unsw.adfa.edu.au/our-trade-china-flourished-despite-cold-war.

124 The agreement entered into force on 20 December 2015. See Department of Foreign Affairs and Trade, 'China–Australia Free Trade Agreement', DFAT, https://www.dfat.gov.au/trade/agreements/in-force/chafta/Pages/australia-china-fta.

125 Stu Woo and Asa Fitch, 'Biden's China Tech Plan: Stronger Defense, Quieter Offense', *The Wall Street Journal*, 11 November 2020, https://www.wsj.com/articles/bidens-china-tech-plan-stronger-defense-quieter-offense-11605102093.

126 Joseph R Biden Jr, 'Why America Must Lead Again', *Foreign Affairs*, March/April 2020, https://www.foreignaffairs.com/articles/united-states/2020-01-23/why-america-must-lead-again.

127 International Monetary Fund, *Expenditure, % of GDP*, IMF DataMapper, https://www.imf.org/external/datamapper/G_X_G01_GDP_PT@FM/ADVEC/FM_EMG/FM_LIDC, accessed October 2020.

128 Scott Morrison, 'In Our Interest: The 2019 Lowy Lecture — Prime Minister Scott Morrison', Lowy Institute for International Policy, 3 October 2020, https://www.lowyinstitute.org/publications/2019-lowy-lecture-prime-minister-scott-morrison.

129 Australian Department of Industry, Science, Energy and Resources, 'Anti-Dumping Commission Archived Cases and the Electronic Public Record', https://www.industry. gov.au/regulations-and-standards/anti-dumping-and-countervailing-system/anti-dumping-commission-archive-cases?field_adc_commodities_tid=All&field_adc_case_type_tid=All&field_adc_country_tid=2062&combine=.

130 John Kehoe, 'Frydenberg Snubs China Dairy Deal', *Australian Financial Review*, 20 August 2020, https://www. afr.com/policy/economy/frydenberg-snubs-china-mengnui-s-600m-dairy-deal-for-lion-20200819-p55n59.

131 See John Edwards, *The Costs of Covid: Australia's Economic Prospects in a Wounded World*, Lowy Institute Analysis (Sydney: Lowy Institute for International Policy, 20 August 2020), https://www.lowyinstitute.org/ publications/costs-covid-australia-economic-prospects-wounded-world. See also James Laurenceson, 'No Wonder China is Confused by Us', *Australian Financial Review*, 25 November 2020, https://www.afr.com/world/asia/no-wonder-china-is-confused-by-us-20201124-p56hlq.

132 See, for example, John Gray, 'Why this Crisis is a Turning Point in History', *The New Statesman*, 1 April 2020, https://www.newstatesman.com/international/2020/04/ why-crisis-turning-point-history; Adam Tooze, 'The Death of Globalisation has been Announced Many Times. But this is a Perfect Storm', *The Guardian*, 2 June 2020, https://www.theguardian.com/commentisfree/2020/jun/02/ end-globalisation-covid-19-made-it-real; and Kenneth Rapoza, 'The Post-Coronavirus World May be the End of Globalization', *Forbes Magazine*, 3 April 2020, https://www.forbes.com/sites/kenrapoza/2020/04/03/ the-post-coronavirus-world-may-be-the-end-of-globalization/?sh=1cfaea7d7e66.

133 World Trade Organization, *COVID-19: Measures Affecting Trade in Goods*, https://www.wto.org/english/ tratop_e/covid19_e/trade_related_goods_measure_e.htm.

It was said that global supply chains would have to be 'shortened' in response to the lack of key medical supplies, which became apparent in the United States in particular. The medical response to the pandemic, however, was overwhelmingly delivered by doctors and nurses and hospitals — medical assets that are not part of international trade or of global supply chains. The material shortages, where they occurred, were in personal protective equipment, testing kits, surgical masks and ventilators. All of these are durable products that could and should be and often were stockpiled by national governments to provide against just such an epidemic. If not enough were stockpiled for that pandemic, the lesson was surely that there should be bigger stockpiles for the next. The time difference between having them in a stockpile and manufacturing them once a pandemic begins is much bigger than the time difference arising from the location of their manufacture, whether Detroit or Shenzhen or Kolkata or some combination of cities in a global supply chain. The size of the stockpile is what matters, not the location of the manufacturer.

Even if it were decided that all countries had to be self-sufficient in the manufacture of surgical masks and ventilators or some other products likely to be required in large quantities during a pandemic, it would make no discernible difference to the vast quantities of goods and services traded internationally if all trade in these particular products ceased completely and for all time. It would not even make much difference to trade in medical products.

But compared to the alternative of stockpiling, self-sufficiency would be complex and hazardous. The manufacture of all these products requires as inputs many other products. The lack of any one of these inputs would hinder the production of the final goods. A country would need to be self-sufficient in all of the product inputs to be self-sufficient in the final product.

134 World Trade Organization, WTO Trade Barometers News Archive, https://www.wto.org/english/news_e/archive_e/wtoi_arc_e.htm; and CPB Netherlands Bureau for Economic Policy Analysis, *World Trade Monitor*, https://www.cpb.nl/en/worldtrademonitor, accessed 1 December 2020.

135 The MPIA is a stop-gap solution in the absence of an operational WTO Appellate Body, allowing participants to benefit from an appeal process in the WTO dispute settlement system. On 31 July 2020, the MPIA named ten arbitrators who will hear appeals of WTO panel reports. See European Commission, 'The WTO Multi-Party Interim Appeal Arrangement Gets Operational', EU News Archive, 3 August 2020, https://trade.ec.europa.eu/doclib/press/index.cfm?id=2176.

136 World Bank, *Exports of Goods and Services (% of GDP)*, https://data.worldbank.org/indicator/NE.EXP.GNFS.ZS.

137 CPB Netherlands Bureau for Economic Policy Analysis, 'Developments in Global International Trade and Industrial Production: August 2020', CPB Memo, 23 October 2020, https://www.cpb.nl/sites/default/files/omnidownload/CPB-World-Trade-Monitor-August-2020.pdf.

138 Federal Reserve Bank of St Louis, *Inflation, Consumer Prices for the United States*, 3 March 2020, https://fred.stlouisfed.org/series/FPCPITOTLZGUSA.

139 It has long been succeeded, even in central banks, by a recognition that the wider measures of money are driven by (or more accurately actually created by) bank lending, and are thus a reflection of changing demand for credit and for goods and services. If demand is weak, inflation will be weak; if demand exceeds supply at current prices, inflation will pick up. That is the proposition behind central bank inflation targeting. Inflation would increase if demand picks up faster than supply. In a global economy, however, where alternative sources of supply are always present, it is less of a risk.

140 John Basquill, 'UNCTAD Eyes "Green Shoots" of Trade Recovery as China Exports Surge', *Global Trade Review*, 28 October 2020, https://www.gtreview.com/news/global/unctad-eyes-green-shoots-of-trade-recovery-as-china-exports-surge/.

141 Statista, *General Motors Company's Vehicle Sales by Key Country in FY 2019*, https://www.statista.com/statistics/304367/vehicle-sales-of-general-motors-by-country/; and Will Feuer, 'Apple Stock Reaches All-Time High after Chinese Government Data Shows iPhone Unit Sales Spike', CNBC, 9 January 2020, https://www.cnbc.com/2020/01/09/apple-stock-hits-new-all-time-high-on-china-iphone-sales-data.html.

142 International Monetary Fund, *World Economic Outlook, Oct 2020: A Long and Difficult Ascent*, IMF, October 2020, https://www.imf.org/-/media/Files/Publications/WEO/2020/October/English/text.ashx.

143 International Monetary Fund, *General Government Gross Debt — Percent of GDP*, 2020, IMF DataMapper, https://www.imf.org/external/datamapper/GGXWDG_NGDP@WEO/EURO/EU/USA/JPN/CHN.

Acknowledgements

Thanks to two anonymous peer reviewers for valuable comments on a draft of this Lowy Institute Paper. Many of the economic issues arising from the pandemic were illuminated in online discussions among the Lowy Institute community of staff and board members. Thanks to the participants in those meetings. Thanks too, to Sam Roggeveen for helpful suggestions on the text and for deftly managing, among his many other responsibilities, the demanding schedule to produce the paper on time and at the agreed length. For her swift, superb edit, I am deeply grateful to Clare Caldwell.

Acknowledgements

Lowy Institute Papers

1. *India: The next economic giant*, Mark Thirlwell (2004)

2. *River at risk: The Mekong and the water politics of China and Southeast Asia*, Milton Osborne (2004)

3. *Unsheathing the Samurai sword: Japan's changing security policy*, Alan Dupont (2004)

4. *Diaspora: The world wide web of Australians*, Michael Fullilove and Chloe Flutter (2004)

5. *Joining the caravan? The Middle East, Islamism and Indonesia*, Anthony Bubalo and Greg Fealy (2005)

6. *Balancing act: Taiwan's cross-strait challenge*, Malcolm Cook and Craig Meer (2005)

7. *The new terms of trade*, Mark Thirlwell (2005)

8. *Permanent friends? Historical reflections on the Australian–American alliance*, Peter Edwards (2005)

9. *Re-imagining PNG: Culture, democracy and Australia's role*, Ben Scott (2005)

10. *Shared secrets: Intelligence and collective security*, Simon Chesterman (2006)

11. *The paramount power: China and the countries of Southeast Asia*, Milton Osborne (2006)

12. *Heating up the planet: Climate change and security*, Alan Dupont and Graeme Pearman (2006)

13. *Pitfalls of Papua: Understanding the conflict and its place in Australia–Indonesia relations*, Rodd McGibbon (2006)

14. *Quiet Boom: How the long economic upswing is changing Australia and its place in the world*, John Edwards (2006)

15. *Howard's decade: An Australian foreign policy reappraisal*, Paul Kelly (2006)

16. *Beyond the defence of Australia: Finding a new balance in Australian strategic policy*, Hugh White (2006)

17. *Mindanao: A gamble worth taking*, Malcolm Cook and Kit Collier (2006)

18. *Second thoughts on globalisation*, Mark Thirlwell (2007)

19. *Australia and Indonesia: Current problems, future prospects*, Jamie Mackie (2007)

20. *Enmeshed: Australia and Southeast Asia's fisheries*, Meryl Williams (2007)

21. *The end of the Vasco da Gama era: The next landscape of world politics*, Coral Bell (2007)

22. *World wide webs: Diasporas and the international system*, Michael Fullilove (2008)

23. *The emerging global order: Australian foreign policy in the 21st century*, Russell Trood (2008)

24. *Into Africa: How the resource boom is making sub-Saharan Africa more important to Australia*, Roger Donnelly and Benjamin Ford (2008)

25. *Zealous democrats: Islamism and democracy in Egypt, Indonesia and Turkey*, Anthony Bubalo, Greg Fealy and Whit Mason (2008)

26. *A focused force: Australia's defence priorities in the Asian century*, Hugh White (2009)

27. *Confronting the hydra: Big problems with small wars*, Mark O'Neill (2009)

28. *China and the global environment: Learning from the past, anticipating the future*, Katherine Morton (2009)

29. *The Mekong: River under threat*, Milton Osborne (2009)

30. *Confronting ghosts: Thailand's shapeless southern insurgency*, Don Pathan and Joseph Chinyong Liow (2010)

31. *Courting reform: Indonesia's Islamic courts and justice for the poor*, Cate Sumner and Tim Lindsey (2010)

LOWY INSTITUTE PENGUIN SPECIALS

1. *Beyond the Boom*, John Edwards (2014)

2. *The Adolescent Country*, Peter Hartcher (2014)

3. *Condemned to Crisis*, Ken Ward (2015)

4. *The Embarrassed Colonialist*, Sean Dorney (2016)

5. *Fighting with America*, James Curran (2016)

6. *A Wary Embrace*, Bobo Lo (2017)

7. *Choosing Openness,* Andrew Leigh (2017)

8. *Remaking the Middle East*, Anthony Bubalo (2018)

9. *America vs The West*, Kori Schake (2018)

10. *Xi Jinping: The Backlash*, Richard McGregor (2019)

11. *Our Very Own Brexit*, Sam Roggeveen (2019)

12. *Man of Contradictions*, Ben Bland (2020)

PENGUIN
SPECIALS

MAN OF CONTRADICTIONS

Ben Bland

A LOWY INSTITUTE PAPER

From a riverside shack to the presidential palace, Joko Widodo surged to the top of Indonesian politics on a wave of hope for change. However, six years into his presidency, the former furniture maker is struggling to deliver the reforms that Indonesia desperately needs. Despite promising to build Indonesia into an Asian powerhouse, Jokowi, as he is known, has faltered in the face of crises, from COVID-19 to an Islamist mass movement.

Man of Contradictions, the first English-language biography of Jokowi, argues that the president embodies the fundamental contradictions of modern Indonesia. He is caught between democracy and authoritarianism, openness and protectionism, Islam and pluralism. Jokowi's incredible story shows what is possible in Indonesia — and it also shows the limits.

PENGUIN SPECIALS

OUR VERY OWN BREXIT

Sam Roggeveen

A LOWY INSTITUTE PAPER

Could Australia have a Brexit moment?

There is a rarely spoken truth at the heart of Australian politics: it is dominated by two parties that voters no longer care about.

Around the democratic West, the public is drifting away from major parties, and politics is becoming hollow. In Europe, populists have been the beneficiaries. In Britain, the result was Brexit.

Australian politics is hollow, too. One of our declining parties could, in desperation, exploit an issue that ties Australia to Asia and which will determine our future security: immigration.

XI JINPING: THE BACKLASH

Richard McGregor

A LOWY INSTITUTE PAPER

Xi Jinping has transformed China at home and abroad with a speed and aggression that few foresaw when he came to power in 2012. Finally, he is meeting resistance, both at home among disgruntled officials and disillusioned technocrats, and abroad from an emerging coalition of Western nations that seem determined to resist China's geopolitical and high-tech expansion. With the United States and China at loggerheads, Richard McGregor outlines how the world came to be split in two.